1001
Pearls of Wisdom

1001

Pearls of Wisdom

Wisdom, wit and insight to enlighten and inspire

David Ross

DUNCAN BAIRD PUBLISHERS
LONDON

1001 Pearls of Wisdom

First published in the United Kingdom and
Ireland in 2006 by:

Duncan Baird Publishers Ltd
Sixth Floor
Castle House
75–76 Wells Street
London W1T 3QH

Conceived, created and designed by
Duncan Baird Publishers

Editorial Consultant: Peter Bently
Managing Editor: Naomi Waters
Editor: James Hodgson
Managing Designer: Manisha Patel
Designer: Allan Sommerville

Commissioned artwork: Sandra Dionisi,
Howard Read and Sally Taylor

British Library Cataloguing-in-Publication Data:
A CIP record for this book is available from the
British Library

ISBN-10: 0-7394-6128-1
ISBN-13: 9-780739-461280

10 9 8 7 6 5 4 3 2 1

Typeset in AT Shannon
Colour reproduction by Scanhouse, Malaysia
Printed in Singapore by Imago

CONTENTS

INTRODUCTION

On one level, wisdom is the name we give to the accumulated knowledge and teachings left to us by our ancestors. But wisdom is also a resource that we can use every day of our lives. In this guise, it is hard to pin down, as it invariably involves a number of elements working in subtle combination. A suitably all-encompassing definition might be: "the ability to think and act with understanding, judgment and insight acquired through knowledge and experience." Put more simply, wisdom is making the best use of available information.

However we define it, wisdom comes from within. As the sixteenth-century French essayist Michel de Montaigne observed, "We can be knowledgable with other men's knowledge, but we cannot be wise with other men's wisdom" (see page 267). It is, above all, our own experience and common sense that help us to make the right decisions, and no book could ever replace our natural instinct to act wisely, if we possibly can. However, what we gain from the wisdom of others is the benefit of another point of view, because, as this book makes clear, great minds rarely think *exactly* alike. A new perspective can help us to tackle a life problem in a way we hadn't considered or it can encourage us to see difficult circumstances in a more positive light.

The idea behind this book is to bring you a rich array of wise words from the great thinkers of the last 3,000 years, who together have made an enormous contribution to human happiness and understanding. Collecting these quotations was an intellectual treasure hunt, and each find felt like a precious discovery. This is why we have called them "pearls" of wisdom. We hope that they will bring you comfort, inspiration, courage, insight, and many other gifts. Some of the quotations may give you answers, but others will raise questions. It's hard to disagree with Albert Schweitzer's assertion that "As we acquire more knowledge, things do not become more comprehensible, but more mysterious" (see page 53).

This is a book intended primarily for browsing – try opening pages at random and see what pearls fall into your laps. However, we have grouped the entries by topic, so that you can also home in on subjects of particular interest.

Most of these themes are as old as the human race, and it is striking how strongly the thoughts of ancient writers still resonate. For example, the Roman politician Cato the Elder's memorably expressed concern for his posthumous reputation (see page 139) has, in fact, helped to ensure his place in posterity. It becomes abundantly clear that the minds of the ancient world had to grapple with many of the same issues that tax us today – for example, the nature of God and our relationship with Him, where to find happiness, and how to lead a worthwhile life. Other subjects, such as conservation and the future prospects of the human race, have assumed greater relevance in modern times, and this is reflected in the larger proportion of contributions from the post-industrial era in these sections of the book.

The pearls in this book not only span many centuries, they also derive from all parts of the world and all the major religious traditions – from Australia to Zimbabwe, Confucianism to Zoroastrianism. It is fascinating to see how thinkers from different cultures go about addressing the universal questions of the human condition.

As well as quotations, which make up the majority of the book, you will find a smaller number of texts introducing a wide range of influential religious or philosophical notions. For example, we have outlined Buddhist ideas such as *dana*, or generosity (see page 26), and *karuna*, or compassion (see pages 97–8), and we have explained the story behind the expression "bringing the mountain to Muhammad" (see pages 53–4). You will also be able to read about philosophical theories such as Plato's Chariot, Occam's Razor and Pascal's Wager. We felt that it was important to offer these pearls of thought, and it was clearer to do so in an explanatory paragraph than in a quotation.

Fishing for pearls can be a time-consuming process. Once, wisdom was available only to the lucky few who benefited from a classical education, who were able to remove themselves from everyday concerns and immerse themselves fully in the works of the "Greats" – notable Greek and Roman philosophers, such as Plato, poets, such as Virgil, playwrights, such as Euripides, and historians, such as Pliny. Today we no longer have to read these books in their entirety to benefit from their authors' insights. Civilization has progressed to such an extent that knowledge that once would have been available only after much painstaking research is just a few mouse-clicks away. The challenge now is not to access the information, but to make sense of it.

We hope that this book will illuminate the world of wisdom and perhaps even encourage you to delve further into some of the writers we have included. But that's for another time.

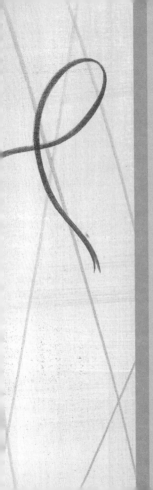

The
Good Life

CONSCIENCE

1   **The all-seeing eye** "In my view whatever is done without display, and without the public as witnesses, is most praiseworthy. Not that the public eye should be entirely avoided, for good actions deserve to be placed in the light; but notwithstanding this, the greatest theatre for virtue is conscience."

MARCUS TULLIUS CICERO (c.106–43 BC), ROME

2   **Clearing a true path** "One who is firm of purpose in a just cause is shaken from his tenacious resolve neither by the clamour of his fellow citizens for that which is unjust, nor by the tyrant's menacing scowl."

HORACE (65–8 BC), ROME

3   **Do the right thing** "It is cowardice to perceive what is right but not to do it."

CONFUCIUS (551–479 BC), CHINA

4   **God in us** "Conscience is God's presence in Man."

EMANUEL SWEDENBORG (1688–1772), SWEDEN

5 **THE STILL, SMALL VOICE**
Conscience sometimes feels like a separate
self, nagging away in our minds – playing
sometimes on our guilt, sometimes on
our sense of responsibility. Whenever we
ignore the promptings of this voice, we are
sacrificing self-esteem – and the inner peace
that it brings – for the sake of some passing
satisfaction. If we can recognize this voice as
a reliable moral compass, we have a better
chance of charting a true course in life.

6 **Divine spark** "… that little spark of celestial fire, conscience."
GEORGE WASHINGTON (1732–1799), USA

7 **Personality testing** "The measure of a man's real
character is what he would do if he thought he would
never be found out."
LORD MACAULAY (1800–1859), ENGLAND

8 **Everything to lose** "Honour has not to be won: it has only not to be lost."

ARTHUR SCHOPENHAUER (1788–1860), GERMANY

9 **The greatest gift** "He that loses his conscience has nothing left that is worth keeping. Therefore be sure you look to that, and in the next place look to your health; and if you have it praise God and value it next to a good conscience."

IZAAK WALTON (1593–1683), ENGLAND

10 **A wild beast**
"Courage without conscience is a wild beast."

ROBERT G. INGERSOLL
(1833–1899), USA

TRUTHFULNESS

11   **Start right** "Even the tiniest initial deviation from the truth is subsequently multiplied a thousandfold."
ARISTOTLE (384–322 BC), GREECE

12   **Trustworthiness** "It is not the oath that makes us believe the man, but the man the oath."
AESCHYLUS (525–456 BC), GREECE

---

13   **OPENNESS**
The great Chinese sage Confucius (551–479 BC) recommended "candour with consideration". It is good to be truthful with others but honesty should be exercised with care, wherever possible using words that are both respectful and sensitive.

---

14   **Sugar the pill** "Speak the truth, but speak it palatably."
SANSKRIT PROVERB

15 **Plain speaking** "The language of truth is always simple and unadorned."

AMMIANUS MARCELLINUS (4TH CENTURY), ROME

16 **Broken promises** "Never breach a covenant, whether you make it with a false person or with a just person of good conscience. The covenant holds for both, the false and the just."

ZOROASTRIAN HYMN

17 **The purity of truth** "Truth is as impossible to be soiled by any outward touch as the sunbeam."

JOHN MILTON (1608–1674), ENGLAND

18 **Poisonous words** "When you step on a snake or brush against it, its venom can kill you. But a slanderer's venom is of another type entirely – it enters one person's ear, yet destroys another."

SANSKRIT VERSE (BEFORE 1000), INDIA

19 **Truth is stranger** "There is nothing so powerful as truth – and often nothing so strange."

DANIEL WEBSTER (1782–1852), USA

---

20 **BE HONEST WITH YOURSELF**
Cant is speech without thought, opinion without knowledge, judgment without evaluation. It is the enemy of true emotion and a clear vision of life. Sincerity, honesty and the simple expression of feeling offer a valuable benchmark to live by.

---

21 **Tell me the truth** "If anyone can demonstrate to me and convince me that I am thinking or acting incorrectly, I will happily change; for I wish to know the truth, which never caused injury to anyone."

MARCUS AURELIUS (121–180), ROME

TOLERANCE

22   **WALKING IN ANOTHER'S SHOES**
Putting ourselves in another person's shoes is the key to empathy and true non-judgmental understanding. Each of us has a unique set of circumstances that make up our lives, and how we are derives from a combination of our conditioning, our innate nature, our experiences, and our environment. But we are all human beings, with the seeds of all human actions latent within us.

---

23   **Moon walk** "Judge no man before you have walked for two moons in his moccasins."
NATIVE AMERICAN PROVERB

24   **Serenity in wisdom** "The growth of wisdom may be measured exactly by the diminution of ill temper."
FRIEDRICH WILHELM NIETZSCHE (1844–1900), GERMANY

25 **Mark of true experience** "All who have actually attained any real religious experience never wrangle over the form in which the different religions are expressed. They know that the soul of all religions is the same and so they have no quarrel with anybody just because he or she does not speak in the same tongue."

SWAMI VIVEKANANDA (1863–1902), INDIA

26 **Selective vision** "A wise man sees as much as he ought, not as much as he can."

MICHEL DE MONTAIGNE (1533–1592), FRANCE

27 **Heresy** "A heretic is a man who sees with his own eyes."

GOTTHOLD EPHRAIM LESSING (1729–1781), GERMANY

---

28 **GOOD MANNERS**
Schools and parents often teach children the importance of manners. However, social niceties, like saying "please" and

"thank you" and eating with decorum, are of limited value unless accompanied by genuine respect for others. It is this underlying civility that gives good manners their true meaning and explains the significance attached to them by educators.

---

29 **The best lesson** "The highest result of education is tolerance."

HELEN KELLER (1880–1968), USA

30 **Eagles and crows** "I am a red man. If the Great Spirit had desired me to be a white man he would have made me so in the first place. He put in your heart certain wishes and plans, in my heart he put other and different desires. Each man is good in his sight. It is not necessary for Eagles to be Crows. We are poor, but we are free."

SITTING BULL (1834–1890), HUNKPAPA SIOUX NATION

31 **Tolerance limits** "We have the right not to tolerate the intolerant. We should tolerate even them whenever we can do so without running a great risk; but the risk may become so great that we cannot allow ourselves the luxury."
KARL POPPER (1902–1994), AUSTRIA/ENGLAND

32 **Truth and reconciliation** "The heart of man is made to reconcile the most glaring contradictions."
DAVID HUME (1711–1776), SCOTLAND

33 **STANDING APART**
The urge to conform is strong in most of us, but if society were entirely made up of conformists, life would be very dull. To be genuinely different and original is a gift to treasure in ourselves and others. It's not easy to be out of step, and not all different ideas are good, but through the ages it is the non-conformists who have stimulated progress.

34 **A different drummer** "If a man does not keep pace with his companions, perhaps it is because he hears a different drummer. Let him step to the music which he hears, however measured or far away."

HENRY DAVID THOREAU (1817–1862), USA

KINDNESS

35   **Gentle rain** "As rain falls equally on the just and the unjust, do not burden your heart with judgments but rain your kindness equally on all."

THE BUDDHA (C.563–C.483 BC), INDIA

36   **Reap what you sow**
"A tree is known by its fruit; a man by his deeds. A good deed is never lost; he who sows courtesy reaps friendship, and he who plants kindness gathers love."

ST BASIL THE GREAT (329–379), ASIA MINOR

37   **It all counts** "No act of kindness, no matter how small, is ever wasted."

AESOP (620–560 BC), GREECE

38 WHY WE SHOULD BE KIND
Plato says that we should be kind "because everyone you meet is fighting a hard battle". One kindness generates others, and from this virtuous contagion we all benefit in a way that helps us face up to our personal struggles.

39 Pass it on "The first thing a kindness deserves is acceptance, the second, transmission."
GEORGE MACDONALD (1824–1905), SCOTLAND

40 A single lovely action "Every man feels instinctively that all the beautiful sentiments in the world weigh less than a single lovely action."
JAMES RUSSELL LOWELL (1819–1891), USA

41 Be good to yourself "When you are good to others, you are best to yourself."
BENJAMIN FRANKLIN (1706–1790), USA

GENEROSITY

42   Good works "To a generous soul every task is noble."
EURIPIDES (480–406 BC), GREECE

43   DANA
For Buddhists, one of the most meritorious acts we can perform is *dana* – charity or generosity. True *dana* means giving freely, with no thought for ourselves, and with a sense of serene joy at the benefit that others will derive from our gift.

44   True charity "True charity occurs only when there are no notions of giving, giver, or gift."
THE BUDDHA (C.563–C.483 BC), INDIA

45   Muck-spreading "Money is like muck: not good unless it be spread."
FRANCIS BACON (1561–1626), ENGLAND

46   **A subtle distinction** "We make a living by what we get, but we make a life by what we give."
WINSTON CHURCHILL (1874–1965), ENGLAND

47   **The golden ladder** "Anticipate charity by preventing poverty; help your fellow man who is in reduced circumstances, either by a substantial gift or a sum of money or by teaching him a trade or by finding him some means of employment so that he may earn an honest living and not be obliged to pursue the grim option of begging for charity. This is the highest rung and summit of the golden ladder of charity."
MAIMONIDES (RABBI MOSES BEN MAIMON) (1135–1204), SPAIN

48   **No limits** "In charity there is no excess."
FRANCIS BACON (1561–1626), ENGLAND

49   **Give and take** "If you desire to take from a thing, first you must give to it."
LAOZI (6TH CENTURY BC), CHINA

50 FORMS OF PATIENCE

At one end of the scale, patience can take the form of the passive act of waiting without agitation or complaint. However, patience can also be linked to action – the painstaking completion of a laborious task or the relentless pursuit of a goal. It takes patience – or persistence – to keep going in the face of rejections or other setbacks, but the prospect of ultimate reward – the satisfaction of success – is a powerful incentive.

---

51 How to deal with unruliness
"Cheerful patience is required both for naughty children and your own mind."

THE BUDDHA (C.563–C.483 BC), INDIA

52 Deferred gratification
"All things come round to him who will but wait."

HENRY WADSWORTH LONGFELLOW (1807–1882), USA

53 **Next to wisdom** "Patience is the companion of wisdom."
ST AUGUSTINE OF HIPPO (354–430), NORTH AFRICA

54 **Long haul** "Patience will bring the snail to Jerusalem."
IRISH PROVERB

55 **Nutcracker** "Dislodging a green nut from its shell is almost impossible, but let it dry and the lightest tap will do it."
SRI RAMAKRISHNA (1836–1886), INDIA

56 **The quickest route** "Hasten slowly and you will soon reach your destination."
MILAREPA (1052–1135), TIBET

57 **A definition** "Genius is only a greater aptitude for patience."
COMTE DE BUFFON (1707–1788), FRANCE

58 **The way of the willow** "Bend like the willow and you can never be uprooted."
YOSHIDA KENKO (1283–c.1351), JAPAN

FORGIVENESS

59 **Lost and found** "Forgiveness is the remission of sins. For it is through forgiveness that what had been lost, and was found, is saved from being lost again."

ST AUGUSTINE OF HIPPO (354–430), NORTH AFRICA

60 **The sterility of vengeance** "Nothing is more costly, nothing is more sterile, than vengeance."

WINSTON CHURCHILL (1874–1965), ENGLAND

61 **WHAT WE GAIN WHEN WE FORGIVE**
According to the Buddha, "we forgive principally for our own sake, so that we may cease to bear the burden of rancour." Genuine forgiveness means developing compassion and understanding toward whoever or whatever caused the hurt – and in doing so dissolving our sense of injury.

62 **First aid for the soul** "Reject your sense of injury and the injury itself disappears."
MARCUS AURELIUS (121–180), ROME

63 **Forgive but do not forget** "The foolish neither forgive nor forget. The naïve forgive and forget. The wise forgive but do not forget."
THOMAS SZÁSZ (BORN 1920), HUNGARY/USA

64 **Wipe the slate clean** "I can forgive, but I cannot forget, is only another way of saying, I will not forgive. Forgiveness ought to be like a cancelled note – torn in two, and burned up, so that it never can be shown against one."
HENRY WARD BEECHER (1813–1887), USA

65 **Greeting a sinner** "Whoever approaches Me walking, I will come to him running; and he who meets Me with sins equivalent to the whole world, I will greet him with forgiveness equal to it."
MISHKAT AL-MASABIH (14TH CENTURY)

66 **Forgive and be forgiven** "It is in forgiving that we are forgiven, for it is in giving that we receive."
ST FRANCIS OF ASSISI (1181–1226), ITALY

67 **How to treat your enemy** "Forgive injuries. Forgive your enemy, be reconciled to him, give him assistance, invoke God on his behalf."
CONFUCIUS (551–479 BC), CHINA

68 **A mother's heart** "The heart of a mother is a deep abyss at the bottom of which you will always discover forgiveness."
HONORÉ DE BALZAC (1799–1850), FRANCE

69 **The ultimate reward** "He who forgiveth, and is reconciled unto his enemy, shall receive his reward from God; for He loveth not the unjust doers."
THE QURAN

70 **Perfection** "Forgiveness is the final form of love."
REINHOLD NIEBUHR (1892–1971), USA

71 **A cost-cutting exercise** "Forgiveness is the economy of the heart ... forgiveness saves the expense of anger, the cost of hatred, the waste of spirits."

HANNAH MORE (1745–1833), ENGLAND

72 **EXTREME FORGIVENESS**
"Sancta simplicitas!" (holy simplicity) were the words of the Bohemian martyr Jan Hus (c.1369–1415) as he saw a devout old woman rush to throw more wood on the fire that was burning him. Even at that moment he could find in his heart the wisdom to understand her unreasoning hatred, and, even more impressively, to forgive it.

73 **Set yourself free** "To forgive is to set a prisoner free and discover that the prisoner was YOU."

MODERN SAYING

Beyond the Veil

TRUTH AND ILLUSION

74 **Neither one thing nor the other** "Things are not what they seem; nor are they otherwise."
SHURANGAMA SUTRA (BEFORE 700 BC)

75 **Two sides of the coin** "Cling to truth and it turns into falsehood. Understand falsehood and it turns into truth. Truth and falsehood are two sides of the same coin. Neither accept one nor reject the other."
RYOKAN (1758–1831), JAPAN

76 **Persuasive words** "A thing is not necessarily false because it is badly expressed, nor true because it is expressed magnificently."
ST AUGUSTINE OF HIPPO (354–430), NORTH AFRICA

77 **The polished mirror** "A person living in a state of delusion is called an ordinary being. But an enlightened person is called a Buddha, who is like a tarnished mirror that gleams like a jewel when it is polished."
NICHIREN (1222–1282), JAPAN

78 **Understanding immortality** "Fools pursue external desires and fall into the wide pit of mortality. The wise understand the meaning of immortality, and do not seek the never-changing in the transient."

UPANISHADS (C.600 BC)

79 **A duty above all others** "It may even be considered better, indeed our duty, to destroy what touches us closely for the sake of upholding the truth, especially as we are philosophers, or lovers of wisdom. For, while both are precious, we are duty-bound to honour truth above even our friends."

ARISTOTLE (384–322 BC), GREECE

80 **RIGHT UNDERSTANDING**
The key to enlightenment, said the Buddha, is right understanding, or seeing things as they are. In Tibetan practice, the path to truth is sometimes summed up as "nothing to do, nowhere to go". A caterpillar does not

"do" anything to turn into a butterfly. When the clouds clear, the sun does not "do" anything to shine. Be who you truly are and enlightenment is within your grasp.

---

81 Advice to a truth-seeker "Rather than continuing to seek the truth, simply let go of your views."

THE BUDDHA (c.563–c.483 BC), INDIA

82 Good seamanship "As a boat on the water can be swept off course by a strong wind, so the intelligence may be carried away by any of the roaming senses on which the mind alights."

BHAGAVAD GITA (1ST OR 2ND CENTURY)

---

83 THE RIVER IN FLOOD
Buddhists believe that all human sufferings and dissatisfactions stem from desire or

"thirst" (*trishna*) – for possessions, sensual pleasures, power, even for wisdom and knowledge – which warps our minds and distorts our understanding. The Buddha compared a life governed by the delusions of *trishna* to a river in flood, sweeping us away to a life of constant discontentment. Learning how to control our cravings is the raft that can carry us over the flood to the opposite shore of insight and peace of mind.

---

84 **Never enough** "When Lord Buddha spoke about suffering, he wasn't referring simply to superficial problems like illness and injury, but to the fact that the dissatisfied nature of the mind itself is suffering. No matter how much of something you get, it never satisfies your desire for better or more. This unceasing desire is suffering; its nature is emotional frustration."

LAMA TUBTEN YESHE (1935–1984), TIBET

85 THE PATHLESS LAND
The Indian mystic Jiddu Krishnamurti (1895–1986) described truth as a land with no paths. There is no single route to perceiving and understanding ultimate reality and we should travel with an open heart and mind. If necessary we should also be prepared to cast off old beliefs that may block us or lead us astray.

---

86 Four corners of truth "Every truth has four corners. As a teacher I give you one corner, and it is for you to find the other three."
CONFUCIUS (551–479 BC), CHINA

87 The unread letter "A dream which is not interpreted is like a letter which is not read."
THE TALMUD

88 Pleasure or happiness? "Pleasure can be supported by an illusion; but happiness rests upon truth."

SÉBASTIEN-ROCH NICOLAS DE CHAMFORT (1741–1794), FRANCE

89 The fundamental delusion "The fundamental delusion of humanity is to suppose that I am here and you are out there."

YASUTANI HAKUUN ROSHI (1885–1973), JAPAN

---

90 "THUS I REFUTE HIM!"
Bishop George Berkeley (1685–1753) denied that matter existed at all. He maintained that material objects exist only through being perceived by us. This would mean that no object existed except when perceived by somebody, but in Berkeley's view, God always perceives everything, and therefore apparently solid objects have what seems to be a continuous existence. Dr Samuel

Johnson, asked what he thought of Berkeley's philosophy, replied by kicking a large stone, as hard as he could. "Thus I refute him!" he said. For Johnson, common sense – and a sore toe – meant more than abstract reasoning.

---

91 **The way of truth** "Refrain from illusions, insist on work and not on words. Patiently search divine and scientific truth."
MARIA KORNILOFF (DIED 1850), RUSSIA

92 **Spiritual arithmetic** "What people usually ask for when they pray to God is that two and two may not make four."
RUSSIAN SAYING

93 **Journey into the darkness** "One does not become enlightened by imagining figures of light, but by making the darkness conscious."
CARL GUSTAV JUNG (1875–1961), SWITZERLAND

94 **Nothing is certain** "The only certainty is that there is nothing certain."

PLINY THE ELDER (c.23–79), ROME

95 **"I THINK, THEREFORE I AM"**
This proposition by the French philosopher René Descartes (1596–1650) has been seen as the first truly modern thought. By forcing himself to reject everything he knew, or thought he knew, unless he could prove it to himself, he found himself reduced to this single truth. This process of systematic doubt was of great importance for the future of scientific and philosophical enquiry.

96 **Private investigations** "By doubting we are led to enquire; by enquiry we perceive the truth."

PETER ABELARD (1079–1142), FRANCE

97 Stranger than fiction
"Fiction is obliged to stick to
possibilities. Truth isn't."
MARK TWAIN (1835–1910), USA

98 Seeing with the heart
"It is only with the heart that one
can see rightly; what is essential
is invisible to the eye."
ANTOINE DE SAINT-EXUPÉRY
(1900–1944), FRANCE

99 Verification process
"All truth passes through three
stages. First, it is ridiculed.
Second, it is violently opposed.
Third, it is accepted as being
self-evident."
ARTHUR SCHOPENHAUER
(1788–1860), GERMANY

100 THE DISMANTLED CHARIOT

A Buddhist teacher, Nagasena, once asked a Greek king called Milinda to prove that he, the king, existed. The king laughed, but Nagasena asked: If you dismantle a chariot piece by piece, can you still call the heap of parts "a chariot"? The heap serves none of the functions of a chariot, so can be one only in name. And when you reassemble the pieces, at what precise point do they become a chariot again? It is impossible to say. So wherein lies its "chariot-ness"? In a sense, the chariot has no intrinsic existence beyond the conventional name we give it and the projections of our minds. The same applies, Nagasena concluded, when we try to pin down the illusory notion of the Self.

101 **There are no such things as good and bad** "Conceptions of good and bad are all mental speculations. Therefore, it is erroneous to say, 'this is good' and 'this is bad'."
CHAITANYA (1486–1583), INDIA

102 **Life is a luminous halo** "Life is not a series of gig lamps symmetrically arranged; life is a luminous halo, a semi-transparent envelope surrounding us from the beginning of consciousness to the end."
VIRGINIA WOOLF (1882–1941), ENGLAND

103 **The eternal present** "In the spiritual world there are no time divisions such as the past, present, and future; for they have contracted themselves into a single moment of the present where life quivers in its true sense. The past and the future are both rolled up in this present moment of illumination, and this present moment is not something standing still with all its contents, for it ceaselessly moves on."
DAISETZ T. SUZUKI (1870–1966), JAPAN

104 **SUBTLE BODIES**
Esoteric and metaphysical traditions of both East and West acknowledge a hierarchy of invisible "subtle bodies", or planes of consciousness, that we possess as well as our solid physical body. Anyone can access these subtle bodies through spiritual practice, eventually ascending to the Light Body, the plane of pure Being – said to be the root of consciousness and the innermost essence of the soul.

---

105 **What is normal?** "The possibility of stepping into a higher plane is quite real for everyone. It requires no force or effort or sacrifice. It involves little more than changing our ideas about what is normal."

DEEPAK CHOPRA (BORN 1947), INDIA/USA

THE UNKNOWN

106 **Fear of the light** "It is easy for us to forgive a child who fears the dark. The true sadness in life is when men fear the light."
PLATO (427–347 BC), GREECE

107 **All will be revealed** "Jesus said: What is hidden from you will be disclosed to you. For there is nothing hidden that will not be revealed. Split a piece of wood; I am there. Raise the stone, and you will find me there."
THE COPTIC GOSPEL OF THOMAS

108 **How religion works** "The efficacy of religion lies precisely in what is not rational, philosophic or eternal; its efficacy lies in the unforeseen, the miraculous, the extraordinary."
HENRI FRÉDÉRIC AMIEL (1821–1881), SWITZERLAND

109 **Seen and unseen** "All things are invisible before birth and invisible again after death. They are seen between two unseens. Why find sorrow in this truth?"
BHAGAVAD GITA (1ST OR 2ND CENTURY)

THE OTHERWORLD
The Celts of the Atlantic coast believed that,
somewhere beyond the western horizon, was
a world not like ours, a land of eternal youth,
untainted by an ordinary life's imperfections.
Only the bravest mortals could enter, and
then only by invitation. Bathed in its clear
light, the mysteries and sadnesses of life
evaporated, replaced by insight and serenity.
The Otherworld remains a powerful symbol

as the destination of a spiritual journey across stormy waters to a haven of understanding and acceptance.

111 **The enchanted land** "All who dwell in Tir na nOg are wise, because here there is no deceit. Truth is not misted over, but is apparent to all. But Truth is a high mountain, and even the Wise may stand at different levels, and obtain a different view."

IRISH MANUSCRIPT, 14TH CENTURY

112 THE POWER OF THE UNCONSCIOUS
Sigmund Freud is often credited with the discovery of the unconscious, the mental store of hidden memories and desires which influence our thoughts and actions in ways we cannot wholly control. But many thinkers before him realized that we have deep resources below the conscious level. The image of the sea is apt: consciousness is the surface, sunlit or cloudy, stormy or calm. Beneath it are depths of varying levels and many dimensions which can be mapped in different ways, but never, perhaps, completely. Meditation can help us explore these regions and make our own inner maps.

---

113 **The deep** "Do you not believe that there is in man a deep so profound as to be hidden even to him in whom it is?"

ST AUGUSTINE OF HIPPO (354–430), NORTH AFRICA

114 **Staring into the abyss** "He who fights with monsters might take care lest he thereby become a monster. And if you gaze for long into an abyss, the abyss gazes also into you."
FRIEDRICH WILHELM NIETZSCHE (1844–1900), GERMANY

115 **The mystery grows** "As we acquire more knowledge, things do not become more comprehensible, but more mysterious."
ALBERT SCHWEITZER (1875–1965), FRANCE

116 **MUHAMMAD AND THE MOUNTAIN**
When asked by sceptics to provide proof of the divine inspiration of his teachings, the Prophet responded by commanding the distant Mount Sala to come to him. But the mountain did not move. Muhammad was not perturbed: "God is merciful," he said. "If the mountain had come, we would have been crushed. Now I will go to the mountain and give thanks to Him." The story is a

rebuke to those who refuse to see a purely spiritual truth and expect faith to be crudely underpinned by physical evidence.

---

117   **Seeing God rightly** "Some people want to see God with the same eyes they see a cow with, and want to love God as they would love a cow. So they love God for the sake of outer riches and inner comfort; but such folk do not rightly love God."

MEISTER ECKHART (1260–1327), GERMANY

118   **The secret of the world** "Nobody, not even the poet, holds the secret of the world."

FEDERICO GARCÍA LORCA (1898–1936), SPAIN

119   **Man or mannequin** "Consider, in good time, that you have something more divine in you than the mechanism of passion, than the strings and tackle of a puppet."

MARCUS AURELIUS (121–180), ROME

120 PHYSICS AND METAPHYSICS

All of the great religions require a belief in the metaphysical (literally, "outside the physical") – that which cannot be understood in physical terms. In contrast, materialists have no time for religion or mysticism. Their classic theory is "dialectical materialism" – the view that everything, including human knowledge and human history, is based on change arising from conflicting material forces in a totally non-spiritual universe. For the materialist, understanding this process of change is the essential thing: the "divine spark" is denied.

---

121   **A materialist view** "Life exists in the universe only because the carbon atom possesses certain exceptional properties."
JAMES JEANS (1877–1946), ENGLAND

VISITATIONS

122 **You are not alone** "When you shut your doors and it is
dark inside, remember never to say that you are alone,
because you are not alone. God is inside with you, and
your guardian spirit is inside with you. And what need do
they have of light?"

EPICTETUS (55–c.135), GREECE

123 **The lamp of the lord** "The human spirit is the lamp of the
Lord, searching every inmost part."

PROVERBS 20.27

124 **A bird in the hand** "He who interrupts the course of his
spiritual exercises and prayer is like a man who allows a bird
to escape from his hand; he can hardly catch it again."

ST JOHN OF THE CROSS (1542–1591), SPAIN

125 **Lasting peace** "There is nothing so lovely and enduring in
the regions which surround us, above and below, as the
lasting peace of a mind centred in God."

YOGA VASISHTHA (DATE UNCERTAIN)

126 **WISDOM OF ANGELS**
Common to the three
great monotheistic
religions, Judaism,
Christianity and Islam,
angels perform a variety
of roles – some bring
messages from God,
others watch over us.
Jacob's dream in the
Book of Genesis
(28.12–16) of angels
travelling between
heaven and Earth by
climbing up and down
a ladder provides a
powerful and heartening
symbol of the possibility
of communication
between worlds.

127 **A guiding hand** "I believe we are free, within limits, and yet there is an unseen hand, a guiding angel, that somehow, like a submerged propeller, drives us on."
RABINDRANATH TAGORE (1861–1941), INDIA

128 **Unseen translation** "If we have listening ears, God speaks to us in our own language, whatever that language is."
MAHATMA GANDHI (1869–1948), INDIA

129 **The life-giving spirit** "I am sure there is a common Spirit that plays within us, yet makes no part of us; and that is, the Spirit of God, the fire and scintillation of that noble and mighty Essence ... Whosoever feels not the warm gale and

gentle ventilation of this Spirit, though I feel his pulse,
I dare not say he lives."

THOMAS BROWNE (1605–1682), ENGLAND

130 **He passes by me, and I do not see him**
"Who alone stretched out the heavens and trampled the
waves of the sea; who made the Bear and Orion, the
Pleiades and the chambers of the south; who does great
things beyond understanding, and marvellous things
without number. Look, he passes by me, and I do not
see him; he moves on, but I do not perceive him."

JOB 9.8–11

131 **The petitioner's reward** "A generous prayer is never
presented in vain; the petition may be refused, but
the petitioner is always, I believe, rewarded by some
gracious visitation."

ROBERT LOUIS STEVENSON (1850–1894), SCOTLAND

THE DIVINE

132   **The eternal quest** "As a deer longs for flowing streams, so longs my soul for you, O God."
PSALM 42.1

133   **Supreme godhead** "My soul dwells joyously with the godhead that is supreme might, supreme wisdom, supreme goodness."
MOTHER JULIAN OF NORWICH (1343–c.1416), ENGLAND

134   **No room for two** "God doesn't easily appear in the heart of a man who feels himself to be his own master."
SRI RAMAKRISHNA (1836–1886), INDIA

135   **YOGA**

In Hindu belief, yoga (literally "yoke") is the name given to various spiritual and physical practices aimed at "yoking" oneself to the Divine. In shedding the transient and the superficial and coming truly into contact with the eternal, it is said that we both renew ourselves and transform our understanding of the world.

---

136   **Do your work in the peace of yoga** "Set your heart upon your work but never upon its reward. Do not work for reward, but never cease to work. ... Do your work in the peace of yoga and free from self-centred desires, do not be moved by success or failure. Yoga is evenness of mind, a peace that is ever the same."
BHAGAVAD GITA (1ST OR 2ND CENTURY)

137   **God within** "I did not find you outside, O Lord, because I made the mistake of seeking outside you who were within."
ST AUGUSTINE OF HIPPO (354–430), NORTH AFRICA

138   **God without** "We can know only one thing about God – that he is what we are not."
SIMONE WEIL (1909–1943), FRANCE

139 **Dark corners** "O Holy Spirit, descend plentifully into my heart. Enlighten the dark corners of this neglected dwelling and scatter there your cheerful beams."

ST AUGUSTINE OF HIPPO (354–430), NORTH AFRICA

140 **Diving for pearls** "There are pearls in the deep sea, but one must hazard all to find them. If diving once does not bring you pearls, you need not therefore conclude that the sea is without them. Dive again and again. You are sure to be rewarded in the end. So is it with the finding of the Lord in this world. If your first attempt proves fruitless, do not lose heart. Persevere in your efforts. You are sure to realize Him at last."

SRI RAMAKRISHNA (1836–1886), INDIA

141 **The dying of the light** "God does not die when we cease to believe in a personal deity, but we die on the day when our lives cease to be illuminated by the steady radiance, renewed daily, of a wonder, the source of which is beyond all reason."

DAG HAMMARSKJÖLD (1905–1961), NORWAY

142 **The unknowable lord** "Each time that something comes to your mind regarding Allah – know that He is different from that! ... No one knows Him in all his aspects. Those who are among the most knowing regarding Him have said: 'Glory to Thee! We have no knowledge except what You have taught us.'"

ABD AL-KADR (1807–1883), ALGERIA

143 **Find the joy of God** "When you surrender all the desires that come to the heart and by the grace of God find the joy of God, then your soul has indeed found peace."

BHAGAVAD GITA (1ST OR 2ND CENTURY)

---

144 **THE COSMIC WORD**
The seventeenth-century German visionary Angelus Silesius asserted that God has, from the beginning of time, uttered only one word. But in that solitary utterance all reality is contained. Today we might liken this

concept to the theory of the all-creating "Big Bang". The Cosmic Word is not available in any human language; indeed, Silesius suggested that only through cultivating silence can we even imagine it.

---

145   **Wonderful quiet** "Silence alone is great; all else is feebleness."

ALFRED DE VIGNY (1797–1863), FRANCE

146   **How to serve God** "Abide in peace, banish cares, take no account of all that happens, and you will serve God according to his good pleasure and rest in him."

ST JOHN OF THE CROSS (1542–1591), SPAIN

147   **A bottomless inkwell** "If the ocean were ink for the words of my Lord, the ocean would be spent before the words of my Lord are spent."

THE QURAN

148 **Heaven and Earth** "The outer world, with all its phenomena, is filled with divine splendour, but we must have experienced the divine within ourselves, before we can hope to discover it in our environment."

RUDOLF STEINER (1861–1925), AUSTRIA/HUNGARY

149 **Earth and heaven** "The splendour of human life, I feel sure, is greater to those who are not dazzled by the divine radiance."

BERTRAND RUSSELL (1872–1970), ENGLAND

150 **The order of things** "Human beings must be known to be loved; divine beings must be loved to be known."

BLAISE PASCAL (1623–1662), FRANCE

151 **Beyond understanding** "A comprehended God is no God."

ST JOHN CHRYSOSTOM (345–407), GREECE

152 **Simple definition** "God is beauty."

ST FRANCIS OF ASSISI (c.1181–1226), ITALY

153   **A God for all seasons** "God is day and night, winter and summer, war and peace, surfeit and hunger."
HERACLITUS (C.540–480 BC), GREECE

154   **Forsake not God** "Forsake not God till you find a better master."
SCOTTISH SAYING

155   **Freedom to worship** "So long as man remains free he strives for nothing so incessantly and so painfully as to find someone to worship."
FYODOR DOSTOEVSKY (1821–1881), RUSSIA

156   **How sweet it is to love** "A great cry in the ears of God is this burning affection of the spirit, which says: 'My God you are my Love: you are all mine and I am all yours. Make me grow in love, that I may learn to taste with the inner mouth of the heart how sweet it is to love and to be melted and to swim in love.'"
THOMAS À KEMPIS (1379–1471), GERMANY

157   ICONS AND ICONOCLASTS
Icons can wield great power. Some native peoples thought that photography stole their souls. Islam at one time forbade any attempt to portray people, in the belief that this blasphemously imitated God's work. Iconoclasm, or image-breaking, has often been a part of religious reform, with the aim of making worship more spiritual. Yet religious art is often of great beauty and power. Problems arise when we worship the visible object rather than the invisible presence that inspired it: in the end, it is the inner vision that matters.

158   Set apart "The act of divine worship is the inestimable privilege of man, the only created being who bows in humility and adoration."
HOSEA BALLOU (1771–1852), USA

159 **Divine progress** "As nations improve, so do their gods."

G.C. LICHTENBERG (1742–1799), GERMANY

---

160 WHY ARE WE HERE?
The idea known as anthropism attempts
to explain why the universe, including our
place within the universe, is as it is. It takes
two forms. Weak anthropism states that the
universe, by its nature, must allow for the
existence of intelligent beings that are
capable of observing it and
philosophizing about it.
Strong anthropism states
that the universe must
have properties that make
the existence of such
beings not merely possible
but inevitable. Anthropism
can be used to support the

idea that the universe shows design, which in turn may help those who try to prove the existence of God.

161 **So many ways** "All the senses, all the forces of the soul and of the spirit, all the exterior resources are so many open outlets to the Divinity; so many ways of tasting and adoring God."
HENRI-FRÉDÉRIC AMIEL (1821–1881), SWITZERLAND

162 **Discoveries** "I searched for God and found only myself. I searched for myself and found only God."
SUFI PROVERB

163 **One with God** "Heaven means to be one with God."
CONFUCIUS (551–479 BC), CHINA

164 **An open book** "I will govern my life and thoughts as if the whole world were to see the one and read the other, for what does it signify to make anything a secret from my neighbour, when to God, who is the searcher of our hearts, all our privacies are open?"

SENECA (4 BC–AD 65), ROME

165 **One and all** "Man is not only a contributory creature, but a total creature; he does not only make one, but he is all; he is not a piece of the world, but the world itself; and next to the glory of God, the reason why there is a world."

JOHN DONNE (1572–1632), ENGLAND

166 **Sacred stones** "A rock-pile ceases to be a rock-pile the instant a single man contemplates it, bearing within him the image of a cathedral."

ANTOINE DE SAINT EXUPÉRY (1900–1944), FRANCE

167 **Proviso** "I have no objection to churches so long as they do not interfere with God's work."
BROOKS ATKINSON (1894–1984), USA

---

168 **THE HUMAN MICROCOSM**
Medieval philosophers believed that human nature "is elevated above all works of God", as Nicholas of Cusa (1401–1464) put it. Created only a little lower than the angels, humankind occupies a central position in the divine order and is a microcosm of all creation. Through our senses we represent the physical world and through our intellect or spirit, the realm of the divine. Between the senses and the intellect comes reason, a bridge between the material and divine worlds.

DEATH AND THE AFTERLIFE _____

169 **Caterpillar tracks** "Just as a caterpillar, when coming to the end of a blade of grass, reaches out to another blade of grass and draws itself over to it, in the same way the soul, leaving the body and unwisdom behind, reaches out to another body and draws itself over to it."
UPANISHADS (C.600 BC)

170 **Nothing to declare** "For we brought nothing into this world and it can be certain that we can carry nothing out."
1 TIMOTHY 6.7

171 **The fruits of your deeds** "Rise early and think upon your deeds, and of the world to come; for you may be certain that the fruits of all your deeds will think upon you."
ANCIENT SANSKRIT VERSE, INDIA

172 **Crossing the divide** "You who have been removed from God in his solitude by the abyss of time, how can you expect to reach him without dying?"
AL-HALLAJ (858–922), PERSIA

173   Unbreakable

"The soul can never be cut
to pieces by any weapon,
nor burned by fire, nor
rotted by water, nor
weathered away by wind."

BHAGAVAD GITA
(1ST OR 2ND CENTURY)

174   A new day

"Death is not extinguishing
the light; it is putting out
the lamp because dawn
has come."

RABINDRANATH TAGORE
(1861–1941), INDIA

175   ATMAN

In Hindu belief, the human soul, or *atman*, is immortal and undergoes rebirth time and again. This cycle ends when we attain a profound transforming wisdom that liberates the soul from the worldly plane and joyously unites it with Brahman, the World Soul or supreme being. Liberation can be reached through a life of unselfish action, the study of ancient teachings, and meditation – but also by a simple and joyful devotion to the divine.

---

176   Vehicle for the soul "Know *atman* as the lord of a chariot; and the body as the chariot itself. Know that reason is the charioteer; and the mind is the reins; the horses they say are the senses; and their paths the objects of the senses."

UPANISHADS (c.600 BC)

177 **Temporary dwelling** "This body is not a home but an inn, and that only briefly."

SENECA (4 BC–AD 65), ROME

178 **Death follows birth and birth follows death**
"Death is as sure for that which is born, as birth is for that which is dead. Therefore do not grieve for what is inevitable."

BHAGAVAD GITA (1ST OR 2ND CENTURY)

179 **A gentle reminder** "Death tweaks my ear. 'Live,' he says, 'I am coming.'"

VIRGIL (c.70–19 BC), ROME

180 **SEEING ETERNITY**
A sense of eternity lies deep in everyone. "I saw Eternity the other night," wrote the visionary Welsh poet Henry Vaughan (1622–1695), "Like a great ring of pure and endless light." Centuries before him,

the Hindu *Upanishads* had stated that the Eternal in humankind cannot die. Today, physics and modern theology seem almost to join hands in a profound and thrilling exploration of a non-material principle that exists beyond time and space.

181 **Relocation package** "That last day does not bring extinction to us, but a change of place."
MARCUS TULLIUS CICERO (c.106–43 BC), ROME

182 **The tadpole and the frog** "For Man to attempt comprehension of the afterlife, is as the tadpole attempting to understand the frog."
JESUIT TEXT

183 **Cause for celebration** "Not by lamentations and mournful chants ought we to celebrate the funeral of a good man, but by joyful songs, for in ceasing to be numbered among

mortals he enters upon the heritage of a diviner life."

PLUTARCH (46–120), GREECE

184 **INTERNAL ALCHEMY**
The term "alchemy" (from the Arabic for "the transmutation") brings to mind images of medieval wizards fruitlessly trying to find a way to turn base metals such as lead into precious gold. However, in the ancient Chinese tradition of Taoism, alchemy – or, more specifically, internal alchemy – takes on a quite different connotation. It involves the transformation of mind and body through meditation and visualization and strict regulation of breathing, diet and sexual practice, as well as through the conduct of a moral life. The aim is to retain life-giving energies, which otherwise ebb away as we approach the end of our mortal existence.

The adept develops an "embryo of immortality" within him- or herself – an immortal, true self, which replaces the physical body.

---

185 **Planning ahead** "Plan for this world as if you expect to live forever; but plan for the hereafter as if you expect to die tomorrow."

IBN GABIROL (SOLOMON BEN JUDAH) (c.1021–c.1058), SPAIN

186 **Follow in their footsteps** "Your lost friends are not dead, but gone before, advanced a stage or two upon that road which you must travel in the steps they trod."

ARISTOPHANES (448–380 BC), GREECE

187 **Night ride** "Dying is a wild adventure, a thrilling gallop through the night of our unknowing. Who can guess what dawn shall bring?"

SAMUEL THORESBY (1850–1921), USA

188 **Scaling down** "O how small a portion of earth will hold us when we are dead, who ambitiously seek after the whole world while we are living."

KING PHILIP II OF MACEDON (382–336 BC), GREECE

189 **Someone at the door** "Pale death with an impartial foot knocks at the hovels of the poor and the palaces of kings."

HORACE (65–8 BC), ROME

190 **DHARMA**

The teachings of the Buddha are known as the Dharma, meaning both "doctrines" and "truth". Buddhists revere the Dharma both as the living embodiment of the Buddha himself, and as a treasure-house of eternal wisdom that opens the path to inner peace and enlightenment. Those who embark on the Buddhist way do so not by professing faith in an omnipotent deity, but by affirming reverence for the Buddha as the greatest of teachers and the Dharma as the truths revealed in his teachings.

191 **The river of time** "Few cross the river of time and are able to reach non-being. Most of them run up and down only on this side of the river. But those who when they know the Dharma follow the path of the Dharma, they shall reach the other shore and go beyond the realm of death."

THE BUDDHA (c.563–c.483 BC), INDIA

192 **Loosely connected** "We are bound to our bodies like an oyster is to its shell."

PLATO (427–347 BC), GREECE

193 **The lover and the beloved** "There comes a time in the seeker's life when he discovers that he is at once the lover and the beloved. The aspiring soul which he embodies is the lover in him. And the transcendental Self which he reveals from within is his Beloved."

SRI CHINMOY (BORN 1931), BANGLADESH

194 **The part that remains** "It is true that when we die a part of us remains – the immortal mind."

HOMER (8TH CENTURY BC), GREECE

195 **Count the days** "So teach us to count our days that we may gain a wise heart."

PSALMS 90.12

196 **Dust to dust** "Why speak of 'death'? Don't make it into some great tragedy, but tell it as it is: 'The time has come for the matter of which you are formed to be returned to the elements from which it came.' Now what is so terrible about that?"

EPICTETUS (55–C.135), GREECE

SACRED HEALING

197   THE HOLY GRAIL
The vessel believed to be either the cup that
Jesus drank from at the Last Supper or the
one that Joseph of Arimathea used to catch
his blood at the Crucifixion has been a source
of inspiration since the Middle Ages.
Guarded in a magic castle, the Grail could
be approached only by someone of perfect
purity. Its mystical powers, including healing,
make the Grail one of the most powerful
symbols of spiritual insight. It emphasizes
the near-impossible challenge of
high ambition: if our finest
aspirations were within easy
reach, they would be less noble.
Another aspect of the Grail wisdom
is that those who try too hard will
never attain success – not worldly
ambition, but only inner peace,
will secure the Grail.

198 **Spiritual cleansing** "Set me free from wicked passions and heal my heart of all inordinate affections, that being inwardly cured and thoroughly cleansed, I may be made fit to love, courageous to suffer, steady to persevere."

THOMAS À KEMPIS (1379–1471), GERMANY

199 **All will be well** "The Lord answered all my questions and doubts: 'I may make all things well; I can make all things well; I will make all things well; I shall make all things well; and you shall see yourself that all things shall be well.'"

MOTHER JULIAN OF NORWICH (1343–c.1416), ENGLAND

200 **Good question** "Why do you hurry to remove anything that hurts your eye, but if something affects your soul you put off the cure until next year?"

HORACE (65–8 BC), ROME

201 **God's people** "You have created us for Yourself, and our hearts are not stilled until they rest in You."

ST AUGUSTINE OF HIPPO (354–430), NORTH AFRICA

202   **Concealed workings** "I am convinced digestion is the great secret to life."
SYDNEY SMITH (1771–1845), ENGLAND

---

203   **THE WHOLENESS CURE**
The sixteenth-century alchemist and physician Paracelsus was way ahead of his time in his belief in observation and research, and in taking an overall view of the patient, not just looking at the disease or symptoms. Holistic medicine accepts the intimate interrelation of parts of the body, and of body and mind. Today's wisdom tends to perceive us not as pure spirit inhabiting a machine-like body, nor as a set of merely physical functions, but as an infinitely complex fusion of the two.

204 **Natural healing** "The art of healing comes from nature, not from the physician; because the physician must start from nature, with an open mind."

PARACELSUS (1493–1541), SWITZERLAND

205 **A divine calling** "In nothing do we more nearly approach the gods than in helping people to be well."

MARCUS TULLIUS CICERO (c.106–43 BC), ROME

206 **Mens sana in corpore sano** "Our prayers should be for a sound mind in a healthy body."

JUVENAL (ACTIVE c.80–c.127), ROME

207 **Helping hand** "Prayer indeed is good, but while calling upon the gods you should lend yourself a hand."

HIPPOCRATES (460–377 BC), GREECE

208   **The best prescription** "A cheerful heart is a good medicine."
PROVERBS 17.22

209   **Wish yourself better** "To wish to be well is a part of becoming well."
SENECA (4 BC–AD 65), ROME

210   **Self-control** "Every human being is the author of their own health or disease."
SWAMI SIVANANDA (1887–1963), INDIA

211   **The foundation of excellence** "When health is absent, wisdom cannot reveal itself, art cannot manifest, strength cannot fight, wealth becomes useless, and intelligence cannot be applied."
HEROPHILUS (C.300 BC), GREECE

212   **Diagnosis** "It is far more important to know what person the disease has than what disease the person has."
HIPPOCRATES (460–377 BC), GREECE

Love and Friendship

SELFLESS LOVE

213 **Love and let live** "The beginning of love is to let those we love be perfectly themselves, and not to twist them to fit our own image. Otherwise we love only the reflection of ourselves we find in them."
THOMAS MERTON (1915–1968), USA

214 **A wonderful thing** "Love is the joy of the good, the wonder of the wise, the amazement of the gods."
PLATO (427–347 BC), GREECE

215 **Break down the barriers** "Your task is not to seek love, but merely to seek and find all the barriers within yourself that you have built against love."
JALAL UD-DIN RUMI (1207–1273), PERSIA

216 **Self-preservation** "Love is union with somebody, or something, outside oneself, under the condition of retaining the separateness and integrity of one's own self."
ERICH FROMM (1900–1980), GERMANY

217 **Never too much** "When we dote upon the perfections and beauties of some one creature, we do not love that too much, but other things too little. Never was anything in this world loved too much, but many things have been loved in a false way, and all in too short a measure."
THOMAS TRAHERNE (c.1636–1674), ENGLAND

218 **Give and receive** "Love grows by giving. The love we give away is the only love we keep. The only way to retain love is to give it away."
ELBERT HUBBARD (1856–1915), USA

219 **THE THREE FORMS OF LOVE**
Ancient Greek, the language in which the New Testament was written, has three words for love. There is eros, the sexual passion we feel for another person, and *philos*, a less intense feeling of affection or friendship. The third form of love, *agape*, is God's fatherly

love for all humankind, as well as our love for God. *Agape* also denotes our feeling of lovingkindness toward all other people, even those we do not know. Whereas erotic love involves the possession of its object, *agape* is a love that gives with no expectation of anything in return.

220　**Be kind** "Put away from you all bitterness and wrath and anger and wrangling and slander, together with all malice, and be kind to one another, tenderhearted, forgiving one another, as God in Christ has forgiven you."

EPHESIANS 4.31–32

221　**Defined by its opposite** "If Love dwelt not in Trouble it could have nothing to love ... Neither could anyone know what Love is, if there were no Hatred; or what friendship is, if there were no enemy to contend with."

JAKOB BOEHME (1576–1624), GERMANY

222 **Beautiful surrender**
"Submit to love faithfully and it gives a person joy. It intoxicates, it envelops, it isolates. It creates fragrance in the air, ardour from coldness, it beautifies everything around it."
LEOŠ JANÁČEK (1854–1928), CZECHOSLOVAKIA

223 **The Sufi way** "A seeker went to ask a sage for guidance on the Sufi way. The sage counselled, 'If you have never trodden the path of love, go away and fall in love; then come back and see us.'"
JAMI (1414–1492), PERSIA

224 **Higher authority** "Who would make love subject to the law? Love is unto itself a higher law."
BOETHIUS (c.480–c.525), ROME

COMPASSION

225   **Rapid relief** "True compassion flows fast, as if we were wounded ourselves, yet without diminishing our strength."
YUKIO KURASAMA (1950–2005), JAPAN

226   **Beyond appearances** "Then cherish pity, lest you drive an angel from your door."
WILLIAM BLAKE (1757–1827), ENGLAND

227   **Calm and kind** "We can be spacious yet full of loving kindness; full of compassion, yet serene. Live like the strings of a fine instrument – not too taut but not too loose."
THE BUDDHA (c.563–c.483 BC), INDIA

---

228   **KARUNA**
The Buddha asserted that spiritual maturity is not possible if we ignore the sufferings of others, whether physical, mental or emotional. The appropriate response to

suffering is to make the most of every
opportunity to show compassion, or *karuna*,
wherever it is needed.

229 **Love the unlovable** "When we come into contact with the
other person, our thoughts and actions should express our
mind of compassion, even if that person says and does things
that are not easy to accept. We practise in this way until we
see clearly that our love is not contingent upon the other
person being lovable."
THICH NHAT HANH (BORN 1926), VIETNAM/FRANCE

230 **Indiscriminate compassion** "How far you go in life depends
on your being tender with the young, compassionate with
the aged, sympathetic with the striving and tolerant of
the weak and strong. Because someday in life you will
have been all of these."
GEORGE WASHINGTON CARVER (1860–1943), USA

231 **Grow your goodness** "I treat as good those who are good. I also treat as good those who are not good. In acting in this way my own goodness increases."
LAOZI (6TH CENTURY BC), CHINA

232 **Tough choices** "One cannot weep for the entire world: it is beyond human strength. One must choose."
JEAN ANOUILH (1910–1987), FRANCE

233 **Make space for yourself** "If your compassion does not include yourself, it is incomplete."
THE BUDDHA (C.563–C.483 BC), INDIA

234 **The meaning of compassion** "I would rather feel compassion than know the meaning of it."
ST THOMAS AQUINAS (1225–1274), ITALY

THE SACRED BOND

235 **A gradual progression** "Love seems the swiftest, but it is the slowest of all growths. No man or woman really knows what perfect love is until they have been married a quarter of a century."

MARK TWAIN (1835–1910), USA

236 **Joined by the elements** "Blow, O wind, to where my beloved is. Touch him and come touch me soon. I will feel his gentle touch through you and see his beauty in the moon. These things are much for the one who loves. One can live by them alone: that he and I breathe the same air and that the earth we tread is one."

RAMAYANA (c.300 BC)

237 **One point of view** "Life has taught us that love does not consist in gazing at each other but in looking outward together in the same direction."
ANTOINE DE SAINT-EXUPÉRY (1900–1944), FRANCE

238 **Rekindling your inner fire** "In everyone's life, at some time, our inner fire goes out. It is then rekindled by an encounter with another human being."
ALBERT SCHWEITZER (1875–1965), FRANCE

239 **THE TRIANGULAR THEORY OF LOVE**
The American psychologist Robert Sternberg (born 1949) developed his "triangular theory of love" as a means of gauging and characterizing the love felt between two people. He measured each person's feelings for the other on three different scales – intimacy, passion and commitment – and gave labels to different forms of love

according to the proportionate importance of these three factors. For example, he categorized a relationship based on intimacy alone as a friendship, one founded on passion as an infatuation, and one in which a couple feel commitment to each other but no passion or intimacy as "empty love". At the other end of the scale, Sternberg described a relationship based on high levels of all three elements as "consummate love", the most complete form of love. However, relationships change over time – the challenge is not only to find consummate love but to sustain it.

240   **Cross-stitch** "Chains do not hold a marriage together. It is threads, hundreds of tiny threads which sew people together through the years."

SIMONE SIGNORET (1921–1985), FRANCE

TRUE FRIENDSHIP

241 **Uninhibited** "A friend is one before whom I may think aloud."
RALPH WALDO EMERSON (1803–1882), USA

242 **Answering back** "A mere friend will agree with you,
but a true friend will argue."
RUSSIAN PROVERB

243 **Chaff and grain** "Oh, the comfort ... of feeling *safe* with a
person – having neither to weigh thoughts nor measure
words, but pouring them all right out, just as they are, chaff
and grain together; certain that a faithful hand will take and
sift them, keep what is worth keeping, and then with the
breath of kindness blow the rest away."
DINAH CRAIK (1826–1887), ENGLAND

244 **Rivers of love** "From small beginnings, they grow stronger
and deeper as they run their course, and once they have
begun they cannot be turned back: Thus it is with rivers,
years, and friendships."
ANCIENT SANSKRIT VERSE

245 **The surrogate** "My best friend is the man who, in wishing me well, wishes it for my sake."

ARISTOTLE (384–322 BC), GREECE

246 **A sunless world** "What sweetness remains in life if you take away friendship? Depriving life of friendship is like depriving the world of the sun. Friendship is the only thing in the world whose usefulness all humankind are agreed upon."

MARCUS TULLIUS CICERO (c.106–43 BC), ROME

247 **Starting point** "Friendship with oneself is all-important because without it one cannot be friends with anyone else in the world."

ELEANOR ROOSEVELT (1884–1962), USA

248 **Testing times** "As yellow gold is tried in the fire, so the true bonds of friendship are seen in adversity."

OVID (43 BC–AD 18), ROME

249   **Our friends define us** "Tell me who your friends are, and I will tell you who *you* are."
ANCIENT ASSYRIAN PROVERB

250   **Nothing is hidden** "Eros will have naked bodies; Friendship naked personalities."
C.S. LEWIS (1898–1963), ENGLAND

---

251   **TEA CEREMONY**
The highly formalized Zen tea ceremony traditionally takes place in a thatched tea house in the host's garden. The separateness of the location helps the participants to isolate themselves from their worldly cares and focus on the intricacies of the serving and drinking of tea. Friends can help each other not only by discussing their problems but by offering a distraction from them.

252   **A bowl of tea** "What is the most wonderful thing for people like myself who follow the Way of Tea? My answer: the oneness felt by host and guest when they meet 'heart to heart' and share a bowl of tea."

SOSHITSU SEN (18TH CENTURY), JAPAN

253   **Wingless wonder** "Friendship is Love without wings."

FRENCH SAYING

254   **More than I deserve** "I no doubt deserved my enemies; but I don't believe I deserved my friends."

WALT WHITMAN (1819–1892), USA

255   **Through the looking-glass** "A friend's eye is a good mirror."
IRISH PROVERB

256   **The simple truth** "The only way to have a friend is to be one."
RALPH WALDO EMERSON (1803–1882), USA

257   **THE SONG OF FRIENDSHIP**
An anonymous poet defined a friend as "someone who knows the song in your heart, and can sing it back to you when you have forgotten the words". True friends are those whose love and reassurance help us to retain a positive belief in ourselves in times of difficulty or self-doubt.

258   **Open the vault** "The greatest good you can do for another is not just to share your riches, but to reveal to him, his own."
BENJAMIN DISRAELI (1813–1881), ENGLAND

SERVING OTHERS

259 **The common good** "What's bad for the swarm is bad for the bee."
MARCUS AURELIUS (121–180), ROME

260 **All things to all people** "May I be medicine for the sick and weary. May I be their doctor and their nurse until the sickness appears no more. May I quell the pains of hunger and thirst with rains of food and drink. May I be a torch for those in need of light, a bed for those in need of a bed, and a servant for those in need of service."
SHANTIDEVA (7TH CENTURY), INDIA

261 **Selective memory** "He who receives a benefit should never forget it; he who bestows one should never remember it."
PIERRE CHARRON (1541–1603), FRANCE

262 **KARMA**
Central to the belief of Hindus and Buddhists is *karma*, the idea that all our actions bring

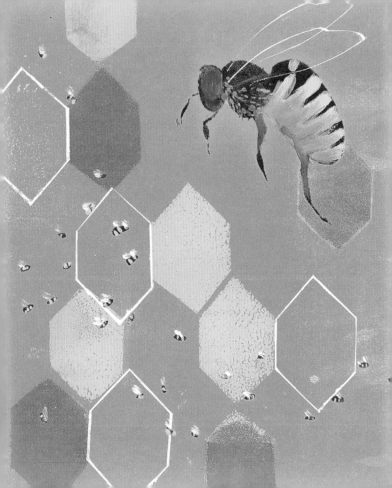

either positive or negative consequences –
or, as St Paul put it, "whatever you sow,
you shall reap" (Galatians 6.7). The key to
avoiding "bad" *karma* is the deep compassion
that arises from knowing that all things in
the universe are interconnected. As Hindu
philosophers have said, the fire of this
knowledge eradicates all *karma*, just as fire
reduces wood to ashes.

---

263   **Loss of pressure** "I have come to understand that if our love
for others suffers a loss of pressure, and becomes merely a
trickle, then our meadows will inevitably shrivel to deserts
and we will choke with a kind of spiritual thirst. This is what
they mean in the East by *karma*."
JANE SONTAG (1920–1999), USA

264   **Harvest time** "Whoever sows to the spirit will from the
spirit reap eternal life. So let us not grow weary in doing

what is right, for we will reap at harvest time, if we do not give up. So then, whenever we have an opportunity, let us work for the good of all."

GALATIANS 6.8–10

265 **An unswerving course** "When you come upon a path that brings benefit and happiness to all, follow this course as the moon journeys through the stars."

THE BUDDHA (C.563–C.483 BC), INDIA

266 **A lifetime's happiness** "If you desire an hour's happiness, take a nap. If you desire a day's happiness, go fishing. If you desire a month's happiness, get married. If you desire a year's happiness, inherit a fortune. If you desire a lifetime's happiness, help someone else."

CHINESE PROVERB

267 **Arbitrate wisely** "If two friends ask you to judge a dispute, do not accept, because you will lose one friend. On the other hand, if two strangers come with the same request, accept, because you will gain one friend."

ST AUGUSTINE OF HIPPO (354–430), NORTH AFRICA

268   **Radiate love** "Just as a flower gives out its fragrance to anyone who approaches or uses it, so love from within us radiates toward everybody and manifests as spontaneous service."

RAMDAS (1884–1963), INDIA

---

269   **THE BODHISATTVA WAY**
In Tibetan and East Asian Buddhism, the supreme embodiment of service to others is the *bodhisattva*, or "enlightenment being" – one who has vowed to devote their entire existence on Earth to the relief of human suffering. The key characteristics of a *bodhisattva* are boundless compassion and lovingkindness, and the first step on the "*bodhisattva* way" is the cultivation of

"awakening mind", or *bodhichitta*, a shift away from self-concern toward concern for others.

---

270 **A selfless prayer** "For as long as space endures, and for as long as living beings remain, until then may I too abide, to dispel the misery of the world. May all the pains of living creatures ripen solely on myself, and through the might of all the *bodhisattvas*, may every being experience happiness."
SHANTIDEVA (7TH CENTURY), INDIA

271 **Advice without strings** "The true secret of giving advice is: after you have given it, to be perfectly indifferent as to whether it is taken or not, and never persist in trying to set people right."
HANNAH WHITALL SMITH (1832–1911), USA

272 **Put on a brave face** "Keep your fears to yourself: share your courage with others."
ROBERT LOUIS STEVENSON (1850–1894), SCOTLAND

273   **A sense of community** "Genuine politics – politics worthy of the name, and the only politics I am willing to devote myself to – is simply a matter of serving those around us: serving the community and serving those who will come after us. Its deepest roots are moral because it is a responsibility expressed through action, to and for the whole."

VÁCLAV HAVEL (BORN 1936), CZECHOSLOVAKIA

274   **Retrospectively** "You will find, as you look back upon your life, that the moments that stand out are the moments when you have done things for others."

HENRY DRUMMOND (1851–1897), SCOTLAND

275   **SERVING THE MAJORITY**
Actions are right in as far as they are useful to, or promote the happiness of, the greatest possible number of people: this was the key idea of the Utilitarian thinkers of nineteenth-century England. They were trying to

understand a world of rapid industrialization, in which people risked being treated as mere commodities. Like all philosophies, Utilitarianism has its limitations – what about the minority of people who are excluded from the benefits of a utilitarian policy and may even be harmed by it? Responsible government must serve all its subjects, not just the majority.

---

276 **Public and private** "Philosophers should consider the fact that the greatest happiness principle can easily be made an excuse for a benevolent dictatorship. We should replace it by a more modest and more realistic principle – the principle that the fight against avoidable misery should be a recognized aim of public policy, while the increase of happiness should be left, in the main, to private initiative."

KARL POPPER (1902–1994), AUSTRIA/ENGLAND

277 **Leadership challenge** "It is not in the nature of politics that the best men should be elected. The best men do not want to govern their fellow men."
GEORGE MACDONALD (1824–1905), SCOTLAND

278 **A premonition** "I don't know what your destiny will be, but one thing I do know: the only ones among you who will be really happy are those who have sought and found how to serve."
ALBERT SCHWEITZER (1875–1965), FRANCE

279 **Return on investment** "The more completely we give of ourselves, the more completely the world gives back to us."
THE BUDDHA (c.563–c.483 BC), INDIA

280 **Be somebody** "One of the greatest diseases is to be nobody to anybody."
MOTHER TERESA (1910–1997), MACEDONIA/INDIA

CIRCLES OF LOVE

281   **Wheels outside wheels** "Come out of the circle of time and into the circle of love."

JALAL UD-DIN RUMI (1207–1273), PERSIA

282   **Unsinkable** "Many waters cannot quench love, neither can floods drown it."

SONG OF SOLOMON 8.7

283   **Our best friend** "Of all the gods Love is the best friend of humankind, the helper and the healer of all ills that stand in the way of human happiness."

PLATO (427–347 BC), GREECE

284   **Thinking for all** "The wise man has no mind of his own. He assumes the mind of humankind."

LAOZI (6TH CENTURY BC), CHINA

285   **Basic requirements** "Love and compassion are necessities, not luxuries. Without them, humanity cannot survive."

TENZIN GYATSO, 14TH DALAI LAMA (BORN 1934), TIBET

286 Emotional cornerstones

"Mutual respect and mutual listening are the foundations of harmony within the family."

THE BUDDHA (C.563–C.483 BC), INDIA

287 A universe of love

"A human being is part of the whole, called by us 'the universe'. Our task must be to widen our circle of compassion to embrace all living creatures and the whole of nature in its beauty."

ALBERT EINSTEIN (1879–1955), GERMANY/USA

291 **SMILING**

"Sometimes your joy is the source of your smile, but sometimes your smile can be the source of your joy," is one of the profound remarks of the Vietnamese Buddhist thinker Thich Nhat Hanh. And not only of our own joy, but that of others. There is no simpler or more expressive way of communicating goodwill than by smiling. Whether or not we know the person to whom we present it, a smile is always a gift worth giving.

---

292   **From me to you** "Try to treat with equal love all the people with whom you have relations. Thus the abyss between 'myself' and 'yourself' will be filled in, which is the goal of all religious worship."

SRI ANANDAMAYI MA (1896–1982), INDIA

293   **Weights and measures** "The injuries we do and the injuries we suffer are seldom weighed in the same scales."

AESOP (620–560 BC), GREECE

294   **A shared purpose** "Those bound in a fraternity of one mind stand stronger than a fortified city".

ANTISTHENES (C.444–C.370 BC), GREECE

295 **Tender, loving care** "The finest qualities of our nature, like the bloom on fruits, can be preserved only by the most delicate handling. Yet we do not treat ourselves nor one another thus tenderly."

HENRY DAVID THOREAU (1817–1862), USA

296 **The world-wide web** "Human action has not woven the web of life: we are but a thread in it. Whatever we do to the web, we do to ourselves. All things are bound together. All things connect."

CHIEF SEATTLE (c.1786–1866), SUQUAMISH NATION

297 **Embodiment of love** "What does love look like? It has hands to help others. It has feet to hasten to the poor and needy. It has eyes to see misery and want. It has ears to hear the sighs and sorrows of humankind. That is what love looks like."

ST AUGUSTINE OF HIPPO (354–430), NORTH AFRICA

298 **Mirror images** "A healthy social life is found only when in the mirror of each soul the whole community finds its reflection, and when in the whole community the virtue of each one is living."

RUDOLF STEINER (1861–1925), AUSTRIA

299 **Lessons in love** "No man is born hating another person ... People must learn to hate, and if they can learn to hate, they can be taught to love, for love comes more naturally to the human heart than its opposite."

NELSON MANDELA (BORN 1918), SOUTH AFRICA

300 **A head for business** "Do not buy the enmity of one man for the love of a thousand men."

AL-GHAZZALI (1058–1111), PERSIA

301 **Change your point of view** "Most people are subjective toward themselves and objective toward all others, frightfully objective sometimes – but the task is precisely to be objective toward oneself and subjective toward all others."
SØREN KIERKEGAARD (1813–1855), DENMARK

302 **The quality of greatness** "I believe that the first test of a really great man is his humility. I don't mean by humility, doubt of his power. But really great men have a curious feeling that the greatness is not of them, but through them. And they see something divine in every other man and are endlessly, foolishly, incredibly merciful."
JOHN RUSKIN (1819–1900), ENGLAND

303 **Citizens of the world** "If it is true what philosophers say of the kinship between god and humankind, then we must all follow Socrates and reply, when asked where we come from, not 'I am an Athenian' or 'I am a Corinthian', but 'I am a citizen of the world.'"
EPICTETUS (55–c.135), GREECE

304 **For the common good** "He does much who loves God much, and he does much who does his deed well, and he does his deed well who does it for the common good rather than for his own sake."

THOMAS À KEMPIS (1379–1471), GERMANY

---

305 **THE GOLDEN RULE**
The world's wisest teachers, from Christ to Confucius, have summarized the ideal of human conduct in a single ethical guideline known as the Golden Rule. It is simply expressed in the traditional proverb, "Do as you would be done by" – treat other people as you would wish to be treated yourself.

---

306 **Nothing more to be said** "What is hateful to you do not unto others. That is the entire law. The rest is commentary."

RABBI HILLEL (1ST CENTURY BC), JERUSALEM

The Maturing Self

SELF-AWARENESS

307 **True self-knowledge** "If we really knew ourselves, we would not have to rely on old teachers."
RYOKAN (1758–1831), JAPAN

308 **The answer within** "At the heart of your being lies your answer. You know who you are and what you want."
LAOZI (6TH CENTURY BC), CHINA

309 **Time to wake up** "O friend awake, and sleep no more! The night is past, would you lose your day also? You have been asleep for countless ages; this morning will you not awake?"
KABIR (1440–1518), INDIA

310 **TOWARD SPIRITUAL MATURITY**
The German philosopher Immanuel Kant
(1724–1804) proposed three ways of
recognizing spiritual "immaturity". According
to Kant, when a book takes the place of our
understanding, or a spiritual director takes
the place of our conscience, or a doctor
decides for us what our diet is to be, then
we are not yet enlightened individuals. You
may have your own criteria.

---

311 **A chance discovery** "As a blind man might come across a
gem in a heap of garbage, in this way the Awakening Mind
appears within oneself."
SHANTIDEVA (7TH CENTURY), INDIA

312 **Double standards** "How shall I be able to rule over others,
that have not full power and command of myself?"
FRANÇOIS RABELAIS (1495–1553), FRANCE

313 **Inner strength** "He who masters others has power.
He who masters himself has strength."
LAOZI (6TH CENTURY BC), CHINA

314 **Behind the mask** "A man never discloses his own character
so clearly as when he describes another's."
JEAN PAUL RICHTER (1763–1825), GERMANY

315 **BREAKING THE BOUNDS**
In the *Sutta Nipata*, the Buddha urges his
followers "to cultivate an unbounded mind,
above, below, and across". How we respond
to situations is often determined by our
habitual patterns of thought. For as long as
these limiting patterns remain, we go on
reacting in the same automatic way time
after time. Recognizing our conditioned
thinking is the first step to stopping the
cycle and breaking through our own self-

imposed boundaries – in order to open the path to imagination, emotional freedom, personal fulfilment and spiritual enlightenment.

---

316   **Personal challenge** "Love yourself and be awake today, tomorrow, always. First establish yourself in the way, then teach others, and so defeat sorrow. To straighten the crooked you must first do a harder thing: straighten yourself. You are the only master. Who else? Subdue yourself, and discover your master."

THE BUDDHA (c.563–c.483 BC), INDIA

317   **Who are we to say?** "We are never so happy or unhappy as we suppose."

FRANÇOIS, DUC DE LA ROCHEFOUCAULD (1613–1680), FRANCE

318   **Be like a sculptor** "Withdraw into yourself and look. And if you do not yet find yourself beautiful, act as does the creator of a statue that is to be made beautiful: he cuts away here, he smoothes there, he makes this line lighter, this other purer, until from his work a lovely face has appeared. So do you also: cut away all that is excessive, straighten all that is crooked, bring light to all that is overcast, labour to make all one glow or beauty, and never cease chiselling your statue, until there shall shine out on you from it the godlike splendour of virtue, until you see the perfect goodness surely established in the stainless shrine."

PLOTINUS (204–270), EGYPT

319 **A world of plenty** "Open your eyes, and you will have plenty of bread."

PROVERBS 20.13

---

320 **KNOW YOURSELF**
In ancient Greece, those who sought the advice of the famous oracle at Delphi were greeted by a simple inscription above the

entrance: "Know Yourself." It was a reminder that as well as seeking the counsel of others we must also look inward at what is going on in our bodies, our feelings, and our minds. By truly understanding ourselves we become our own surest guides.

---

321 **Unseen wonders** "People travel to wonder at the height of mountains, at the huge waves of the sea, at the long courses of rivers, at the vast compass of the ocean, at the circular motion of the stars; and they pass by themselves without wondering."
ST AUGUSTINE OF HIPPO (354–430), NORTH AFRICA

322 **Concentrate on self** "When you encounter someone more able than you, think about becoming their equal. When you encounter someone less able than you, turn your thoughts inward and examine yourself."
CONFUCIUS (551–479 BC), CHINA

323 **Trust yourself** "As soon as you trust yourself,
you will know how to love."

JOHANN WOLFGANG VON GOETHE (1749–1832), GERMANY

324 **What you are** "You don't have a soul. You are a Soul.
You have a body."

C.S. LEWIS (1898–1963), ENGLAND

325 **A natural response** "We can't help being thirsty, moving
toward the voice of water."

JALAL AD-DIN RUMI (1207–1273), PERSIA

326 **Could do better** "What is terrible is to pretend that the
second-rate is first rate, that you don't need love when you
do or that you like your work, when you know quite well
you're capable of better."

DORIS LESSING (BORN 1919), ENGLAND

327   **Flight from the self** "I pack my trunk, embrace my friends, embark on the sea, and at last wake up in Naples, and there beside me is the Stern Fact, the Sad Self, unrelenting, identical, that I fled from."

RALPH WALDO EMERSON (1803–1882), USA

328   **Sudden transition** "The minute a man is convinced he's interesting, he isn't."

STEPHEN LEACOCK (1869–1944), CANADA

329   **A rare breed**

"Most can see other people's faults. A few can see other people's virtues. And two or three can even see their own shortcomings."

ANCIENT SANSKRIT VERSE

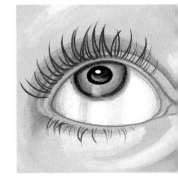

SELF-ESTEEM

330 **Impossible odds** "If I have lost confidence in myself, I have the universe against me."

RALPH WALDO EMERSON (1803–1882), USA

331 **AN EVEN TEMPERATURE**
The Buddha once told one of his followers: "You yourself, as much as anybody in the entire universe, deserve your love and affection." The praise of others is most welcome when it crowns rather than bolsters our self-worth. When our sense of our own value depends on the views of others, it slips out of our control, rising and falling like the thread of mercury in a thermometer.

332 **Audience reaction** "To seek all your applause from outside yourself is to have your happiness in another's keeping."

CLAUDIUS CLAUDIANUS (340–410), EGYPT

333 **Be kind to yourself** "Do not be a harsh judge of yourself. Without kindness toward ourselves we cannot love the world."
THE BUDDHA (c.563–c.483 BC), INDIA

334 **In memoriam** "After I am dead I would rather people wonder why I do not have a monument than why I do have one."
CATO THE ELDER (234–149 BC), ROME

335 **Inevitable critics** "Few men have been admired by their own servants."
MICHEL DE MONTAIGNE (1533–1592), FRANCE

336 **Unrepeatable** "At bottom every man knows well enough that he is a unique being, only once on this earth; and by no extraordinary chance will such a marvellously picturesque piece of diversity in unity as he is ever be put together a second time."
FRIEDRICH WILHELM NIETZSCHE (1844–1900), GERMANY

337 PUBLISH AND BE DAMNED
When a blackmailer tried to extort money
from the first Duke of Wellington to cover up
a disreputable aspect of his past, the duke's
response was: "Publish, and be damned." He
had enough confidence in himself not to be
swayed by this threat to his good name. Sure
enough, his reputation remained unsullied,
and indeed he won respect for allowing
the story to be known. He knew that the
blackmailer lives off fear, and if one shows
no fear, a blackmailer is powerless.

---

338 Vicious circle "We have nothing to fear but fear itself."
FRANKLIN D. ROOSEVELT (1882–1945), USA

339 Never be satisfied "Show me a thoroughly satisfied man
and I will show you a failure."
THOMAS EDISON (1847–1931), USA

340   **A wretched state** "To be pleased with one's limits is a wretched state."

JOHANN WOLFGANG VON GOETHE (1749–1832), GERMANY

341   **EVERY DAY, IN EVERY WAY, I EXCEL MYSELF** One of the remarkable attributes of our minds is that they can work on themselves. The French pharmacist Emile Coué (1857–1926), who was skilled as a hypnotist, developed the idea of "auto-suggestion", in which a thought, if taken to heart and repeated to oneself on a regular basis, eventually becomes a firmly established aspect of personality. Auto-suggestion is more than a reminder to do something: it brings about an actual change in our mental landscape.

342 **An overrated virtue** "Modesty is the lowest of the virtues, and is a real confession of the deficiency it indicates. He who undervalues himself is justly undervalued by others."
WILLIAM HAZLITT (1778–1830), ENGLAND

343 **False modesty** "One may be humble out of pride."
MICHEL DE MONTAIGNE (1533–1592), FRANCE

344 **Questions of identity** "If I am not for me, who is for me? And being for me, what am I?"
RABBI HILLEL (1ST CENTURY BC), JERUSALEM

345 **Inside story** "Everyone has inside of him a piece of good news. The good news is that you don't know how great you can be! How much you can love! What you can accomplish! And what your potential is!"
ANNE FRANK (1929–1945), GERMANY

ACCEPTANCE

346   **Adapting to change** "In our lives, change is unavoidable, loss is unavoidable. In the adaptability and ease with which we experience change lie our happiness and freedom."
THE BUDDHA (c.563–c.483 BC), INDIA

347   **Never condemn** "We cannot change anything until we accept it. Condemnation does not liberate: it oppresses."
CARL GUSTAV JUNG (1875–1961), SWITZERLAND

348   **Acceptance – and action** "What is done for you – allow it to be done. What you must do yourself – make sure you do it."
IBRAHIM IBN AL-KHAWWAS (9TH CENTURY), IRAQ

349   **Against the grain** "Of all the dangerous energies that can breed inside our minds, one of the most harmful to our contentment is the wish that things were otherwise. By an exertion of effort we can attempt to change the way other people think or behave, or the way that circumstances are evolving, but when that effort encounters resistance, as it often will, corrosive chemicals start to eat away at the core of our being. Even the extent to which we can modify our own characters is debatable: perhaps all we can do is commit to a program of action that goes against the grain of those tendencies in ourselves that we most heartily dislike."

JAMES HOOVER (BORN 1943), CANADA

350 Unanswered prayers "More tears are shed over answered prayers than unanswered ones."

ST TERESA OF AVILA (1515–1582), SPAIN

351 Let's face the music ... "Worry comes from not facing unpleasant possibilities."

BERTRAND RUSSELL (1872–1970), ENGLAND

352 ... and dance "We're fools whether we dance or not; so we might as well dance."

JAPANESE PROVERB

353 **THE PRESENT MOMENT**
The German thinker Eckhart Tolle (born 1948) advised us in his book *The Power of Now* that the present moment is all we ever have. Tolle's view is that to gain serenity we must live in the present, and to do this we must learn to conquer the destructiveness of the mind, which is constantly reaching forward and backward in time.

---

354 **Healthy living** "The secret of health for both mind and body is not to mourn for the past, worry about the future, or anticipate troubles, but to live in the present moment wisely and earnestly."

THE BUDDHA (c.563–c.483 BC), INDIA

355 **Maximum contrast** "Sorrows remembered sweeten present joy."

ROBERT POLLOK (1799–1827), SCOTLAND

356 **Weatherproof** "The best thing one can do when it's raining is to let it rain."
HENRY WADSWORTH LONGFELLOW (1807–1882), USA

357 **While the sun shines**
"Take what the gods give while their hands are open, for none knows what they will withhold when they are shut."
AFRICAN PROVERB

358 **The jewel of adversity** "Sweet are the uses of adversity, which, like a toad, though ugly and venomous, wears yet a precious jewel in its head."
WILLIAM SHAKESPEARE (1564–1616), ENGLAND

359 **The rarest wisdom** "The teaching that is without words, the gain that is to be had from letting all things take their course: these surpass the understanding of all but a very few."
LAOZI (6TH CENTURY BC), CHINA

360 **TWO VIEWS OF ENLIGHTENMENT**
Western thinkers traditionally mean by
enlightenment the triumph of reason
(over, for example, self-gratification, sin,
tradition or prejudice), whereas Eastern
sages habitually use the term to mean
the soul's triumph over reason, as in the
Buddha's moment of enlightenment under
the Bodhi Tree. The one places emphasis
on understanding, the other on acceptance.
Many now seek to harmonize the two.

---

361 **The serenity prayer** "God, give us the serenity to accept
what cannot be changed; Give us courage to change what
should be changed; Give us the wisdom to distinguish one
from the other."

REINHOLD NIEBUHR (1892–1971), USA

FATE, LUCK AND CHANCE

362 **Do we make our own luck?** "I'm a great believer in luck, and I find the harder I work the more I have of it."

THOMAS JEFFERSON (1743–1826), USA

363 **FREE WILL VERSUS DESTINY**
This topic has fuelled many a passionate debate – does God, or the Universe, give us complete freedom to think, decide and do, or is every thought and action predetermined? Many great thinkers, such as Benedict de Spinoza (1632–1677), have denied the existence of chance and free will, deeming everything that happens to be already contained within the mind of God. Others, such as Henri Bergson (1859–1941), have argued that the struggle between Life and Matter is essentially and eternally creative and that new, unplanned, unpredictable things can and must happen.

364   **Free to do as God wills** "God does not compel the will: rather He sets the will free, so that it wills not otherwise than what God himself wills."
MEISTER ECKHART (1260–1327), GERMANY

365   **The garland** "God gives you a garland made of all the good and bad that you have done in previous lives. You have been born with that garland round your neck."
BHAGAVAN SRI SATHYA SAI BABA (BORN 1926), INDIA

366   **Riding the waves** "Do not fear to take chances. When it is making headway, a boat may rock."
CHINESE PROVERB

367   **Message for the downtrodden** "Chance has never yet satisfied the hope of a suffering people. Action, self-reliance, the vision of self and the future have been the only means by which the oppressed have seen and realized the light of their own freedom."
MARCUS GARVEY (1887–1940), JAMAICA

368 **Into thin air** "If people never vanished like the dew of Adashino, never disappeared like the smoke over Toribeyama, how little power to move us could anything possess. The most precious thing about life is its uncertainty."

YOSHIDA KENKO (1283–c.1351), JAPAN

369 **No accident** "The order of the world is no accident ... The religious insight is the grasp of this truth."

ALFRED NORTH WHITEHEAD (1861–1947), ENGLAND

370 **The birds of sadness** "You cannot prevent the birds of sadness from flying over your head, but you can prevent them from nesting in your hair."

CHINESE PROVERB

371 **Spirit of adventure** "For believe me: the secret for harvesting from existence the greatest fruitfulness and greatest enjoyment is – to live dangerously."

FRIEDRICH WILHELM NIETZSCHE (1844–1900), GERMANY

372   **A meaningful future** "Promises are the uniquely human way of ordering the future, making it predictable and reliable to the extent that this is humanly possible."
HANNAH ARENDT (1906–1975), GERMANY/USA

373   **Pleasant surprises** "One should accept nectar even if it comes from poison and gold even if it comes from dirt."
CHANAKYA PANDITA (350–275 BC), INDIA

374   **Safe expectations** "Be prudent in trusting both yourself and others and you will be joyful when things go well and not lament when they go badly."
YOSHIDA KENKO (1283–c.1351), JAPAN

---

375   **THE ORACLE SPEAKS**
The Oracle of Delphi, in ancient Greece, was visited by many in search of an answer to their problems or an assurance about the

future. But often the answer was ambiguous. Philip of Macedon, father of Alexander the Great, was told that his war against the Persians would destroy a great empire. Philip set off boldly, but the empire that fell was his own. A truth may resemble its opposite.

---

376 **Expect the unexpected** "What we anticipate seldom occurs; what we least expect generally happens."

BENJAMIN DISRAELI (1804–1881), ENGLAND

377 **Power of the word** "As long as a word remains unspoken, you are its master; once you utter it, you are its slave."

IBN GABIROL (SOLOMON BEN JUDAH) (c.1021–c.1058), SPAIN

378 **Against prevarication** "The risk of an incorrect decision is nothing compared to the terror of indecision."

MAIMONIDES (RABBI MOSES BEN MAIMON) (1135–1204), SPAIN

379 **Right here, right now** "You cannot run away from weakness; you must some time fight it out or perish; and if that be so, why not now, and where you stand?"
ROBERT LOUIS STEVENSON (1850–1894), SCOTLAND

380 **Come what may** "Whatever you have in your mind – forget it; whatever you have in your hand – give it; whatever is to be your fate – face it!"
ABU SA'ID (DIED 1049), PERSIA

381 **Faith of the fisherman** "Luck affects everything. Keep your hook cast at all times. In the water where you least expect it there will be a fish."
OVID (43 BC–AD 18), ROME

FINDING STILLNESS

382   **BEING MINDFUL**
At the heart of all Buddhist practice is the cultivation of "mindfulness" – the direction of one's full attention to a single object or activity, such as breathing or walking, or preparing a meal, for a sustained period of time. By this means we counter the mind's tendency to dart off distractedly in random directions. Only after stilling the mind like this can the Buddhist progress to more advanced forms of meditation and derive insights into the nature of self and reality.

---

383   **The day ahead** "Agenda for today: breathe out, breathe in, breathe out."
THE BUDDHA (C.563–C.483 BC), INDIA

384   **Judge not** "It is within our power not to make a judgment about something, and so not to disturb our minds; for

nothing in itself possesses the power to form our judgments."
MARCUS AURELIUS (121–180), ROME

385 Pride fears its fall "The wise esteem the contempt of the
arrogant more than the elixir of the gods. Humility sleeps
soundly at night. Pride lies awake, fearing its own downfall."
ANCIENT SANSKRIT VERSE

386 Temperature control "Activity conquers coldness.
Stillness conquers heat."
LAOZI (6TH CENTURY BC), CHINA

387 Peace aids digestion "Better is a dry morsel with quiet than
a house full of feasting with strife."
PROVERBS 107.1

388 Wild horses "When you lack understanding and are unable
to control your mind, your senses do not obey you, just as
unruly horses do not obey a charioteer."
UPANISHADS (C.600 BC)

389 **Time management** "Take care of each moment and you take care of all time."

THE BUDDHA (c.563–c.483 BC), INDIA

390 **Stop worrying** "Those who are always preoccupied with something cannot enjoy the world."

LAOZI (6TH CENTURY BC), CHINA

391 **Still waters** "If water derives clarity from stillness, how much more so does the mind! The mind of the sage, being in repose, becomes the mirror of the universe, the speculum of all creation."

ZHUANGZI (c.369–286 BC), CHINA

392 **The way of independence** "If you will discipline yourself to make your mind self-sufficient you will thereby be least vulnerable to injury from the outside."

CRITIAS OF ATHENS (c.460–403 BC), GREECE

393   **Let thoughts pass** "Thoughts of themselves have no substance; let them arise and pass away unheeded. Thoughts will not take form of themselves, unless they are grasped by the attention; if they are ignored, there will be no appearing and no disappearing."

ASHVAGHOSHA (1ST CENTURY), INDIA

---

394   **TRAVEL WITHIN**
According to the Roman writer Horace, "Those who take flight across the seas change their skies but not their souls." It is often tempting to seek inner peace by changing our surroundings, but wherever we may go, we always carry the baggage of our own thoughts and feelings. As Horace observed, the true journey to contentment and tranquillity is a voyage of self-knowledge.

395 **Self-mastery** "Before you take another step, step back into yourself. If you can govern yourself and be your own master, yours is the whole wide world and everything within it."
PAUL FLEMING (1609–1640), GERMANY

396 **Focus on the act** "When rising, standing, walking, performing any action, or stopping, you should constantly focus your mind on the act and the doing of it, not on your relationship to the act or its character or value ... You should simply practice focusing on the act itself, understanding it to be an expedient means for attaining tranquillity of mind, realization, insight and wisdom."
ASHVAGHOSHA (1ST CENTURY), INDIA

397 **The odd couple** "Fame and tranquillity can never be bedfellows."
MICHEL DE MONTAIGNE (1533–1592), FRANCE

398 **The cost of emotion** "Anger is an expensive luxury."
POPE ST GREGORY THE GREAT (c.540–604), ROME

399 **SOLITUDE AND SOCIETY**
Through the ages, thinking people have
been torn between the attractions of
solitary contemplation and the pleasure
of sharing ideas with others. Wisdom comes
in different forms. The meditative wisdom
of St Anthony or a Buddhist *bodhisattva*
("enlightenment being") and the social
wisdom of Socrates or St Benedict are both
of great value. A combination of the two is
ideal, just as we need both food and drink.
Most of us could benefit from more time
spent alone, not least to reflect on the
quality and personal value of what we
gain from others.

---

400 **In combination** "Solitude is as needful to the imagination
as society is wholesome for the character."
JAMES RUSSELL LOWELL (1819–1891), USA

401 **Depths and shallows** "Silence is deep as Eternity; speech is shallow as Time."
THOMAS CARLYLE (1795–1881), SCOTLAND

402 **A peaceful place** "Commune with your own heart, and in your chamber, and be still."
BOOK OF COMMON PRAYER (1662), ENGLAND

403 **Careful nurturing** "Detachment is a plant of slow growth; if you pluck the tender plant to look for the pods, you will be disappointed. So too, long and constant practice alone is rewarded by the Peace that God offers. "
BHAGAVAN SRI SATHYA SAI BABA (BORN 1926), INDIA

404 **The eye of the storm** "Do not lose your inner peace for anything whatsoever, even if the whole world seems tumbled down."
ST FRANÇOIS DE SALES (1567–1622), FRANCE

405 **A noble pose** "In meditating, sit with the dignity of a king or queen, and stay centred in this dignity as you pass through the day."
THE BUDDHA (c.563–c.483 BC), INDIA

406 **Keeping busy** "Though I am always in haste, I am never in a hurry."
JOHN WESLEY (1703–1791), ENGLAND

407 **Total stillness** "This they call the highest state: when the five senses and the mind are still, when not even reason stirs."
UPANISHADS (c.600 BC)

FAITH, HOPE AND COMMITMENT

408 **Our potential** "If you find a thing difficult, consider whether it would be possible for any person to do it. Because anything that is humanly possible, that falls within human capabilities – you too can accomplish."
MARCUS AURELIUS (121–180), ROME

409 **Ever forward** "The only limit to our realization of tomorrow will be our doubts of today. Let us move forward with strong and active faith."
FRANKLIN D. ROOSEVELT (1882–1945), USA

410 **Taming the elephant** "Small things grow mighty, if they are skillfully combined. Blades of grass will make a rope to bind a raging elephant."
HITOPADESHA (14TH CENTURY), INDIA

411 **Seeing and believing** "Faith is to believe what we do not see; and the reward of this faith is to see what we believe. By faith we are collected and wound up into unity within

ourselves, having been scattered in multiplicity."

ST AUGUSTINE OF HIPPO (354–430), NORTH AFRICA

412   **Choose your weapon wisely** "If we fight with faith we are twice armed."

PLATO (427–347 BC), GREECE

413   **Strength without numbers** "One man with courage makes a majority."

ANDREW JACKSON (1767–1845), USA

414   **Building the dream** "If you have built castles in the air, your work need not be lost; that is where they should be. Now put the foundations under them."

HENRY DAVID THOREAU (1817–1862), USA

415   **The art of change** "Habit is habit and not to be flung out of the window by any man, but coaxed downstairs a step at a time."

MARK TWAIN (1835–1910), USA

416   **The castle of convictions** "One needs to be slow to form convictions, but once formed they must be defended against the heaviest odds."
MAHATMA GANDHI (1869–1948), INDIA

417   **The soft option** "It is easier to fight for one's principles than to live up to them."
ALFRED ADLER (1870–1937), AUSTRIA

418   **Hope sustains us** "The pillar of the world is hope."
KANURI PROVERB, NIGERIA

419   **Chemistry lesson** "There is no hope unmixed with fear, and no fear unmixed with hope."
BENEDICT DE SPINOZA (1632–1677), HOLLAND

420   **Heart and mind** "We do not believe in immortality because we can prove it, but we try to prove it because we cannot help believing it."
HARRIET MARTINEAU (1802–1876), ENGLAND

421 **A priceless gift** "Faith is an excitement and an enthusiasm: it is a condition of intellectual magnificence to which we must cling as to a treasure, and not squander on our way through life in the small coin of empty words, or in exact and priggish argument."

GEORGE SAND (1804–1876), FRANCE

422 **Small is strong** "Be faithful in small things: it is in them that your strength lies."

MOTHER TERESA (1910–1997), MACEDONIA/INDIA

423 **A thought away** "Whoever reflects earnestly on the meaning of life is on the verge of an act of faith."

PAUL TILLICH (1886–1965), USA

424 **A trick of the light** "It is our own mental attitude which makes the world what it is for us. Our thoughts make things beautiful, our thoughts make things ugly. The whole world is in our own minds. Learn to see things in the proper light. First, believe in this world – that there is meaning behind everything. Everything in the world is good, is holy and beautiful. If you see something evil, think that you are not understanding it in the right light. Throw the burden on yourselves!"

SWAMI VIVEKANANDA (1863–1902), INDIA

425 **Living possibility** "Hope is a waking dream."

ARISTOTLE (384–322 BC), GREECE

426 **PASCAL'S WAGER**
With pragmatic logic, Blaise Pascal (1623–1662) proposed this reason for belief in a Creator: it is better to believe in God than disbelieve. For if there is no God, it

does not matter if you were wrong. But if there is a God, it would matter very much if you were wrong. Therefore, the only fail-safe attitude is belief. This reasoning has sometimes been seen as cynical, but Pascal was no cynic. To him, if there was no God, there was nothing – the universe would make no sense.

---

427 **The path of faith** "If a man wishes to be sure of the road he treads on, he must close his eyes and walk in the dark."
ST JOHN OF THE CROSS (1542–1591), SPAIN

428 **Put to the test** "I cannot praise a fugitive and cloistered virtue … that never sallies out and sees her adversary, but slinks out of the race, where that immortal garland is to be run for, not without dust and heat."
JOHN MILTON (1608–1674), ENGLAND

429   **Persistence and determination** "Nothing in the world can take the place of persistence. Persistence and determination are omnipotent."
CALVIN COOLIDGE (1872–1933), USA

430   **A recipe for happiness** "Three grand essentials to happiness in this life are something to do, something to love, and something to hope for."
JOSEPH ADDISON (1672–1719), ENGLAND

431   **Hidden benefits** "Pray inwardly, even if you do not enjoy it. It does good, though you feel nothing. Yes, even though you think you are doing nothing."
MOTHER JULIAN OF NORWICH (1343–c.1416), ENGLAND

MODERATION

432 **THE MIDDLE WAY**

"Compassion and inner peace are precious things, easily lost through intoxication." This advice given by the Buddha to his followers 2,500 years ago has a resonance for us today. In a self-centred and over-stimulated age it is easy to lose contact with our true, inner selves, and to be insensitive to others. But it does not follow that we must lead the life of an ascetic. The Buddha himself recommended the "Middle Way", a path of moderation that rejected both sensory indulgence and extreme mortification.

---

433 **Resist passion** "Those who are susceptible to passion experience much misery and little enjoyment, like a cow snatching at wisps of grass as it pulls its heavy load."

THE BUDDHA (c.563–c.483 BC), INDIA

434 **The tree of temperance** "The truly temperate man sets himself apart like a tree in a sunny field: it prospers, its yield is doubled, its fruit is sweet, its shadows pleasing, and it is fated one day to become a fine monument."
TEACHING OF AMENEMIPET (C.700 BC), EGYPT

435 **A string of pearls** "Moderation is the silken string running through the pearl chain of all virtues."
BISHOP HALL (1574–1656), ENGLAND

436 **The source of moderation** "Moderation, which consists in an indifference about little things, and in a prudent and well-proportioned zeal about things of importance, can proceed from nothing but true knowledge, which has its foundation in self-acquaintance."
PLATO (427–347 BC), GREECE

437 **An elusive balance** "Complete abstinence is easier than perfect moderation."
ST AUGUSTINE OF HIPPO (354–430), NORTH AFRICA

438 **Sense of proportion** "Consider how the suffering caused by your anger and grief is often much greater than the suffering caused by the very things for which you are angry and aggrieved."
MARCUS AURELIUS (121–180), ROME

439 **Self-sufficiency** "The man who makes everything that leads to happiness depend upon himself, and not upon other men, has adopted the very best plan for living happily. This is the man of moderation, the man of manly character and of wisdom."
PLATO (427–347 BC), GREECE

440 **Checks and balances** "If passion drives you, let reason hold the reins."
BENJAMIN FRANKLIN (1706–1790), USA

441 **Effective communication** "Many will remember the words of a fair youth who speaks little, but agreeably."
YOSHIDA KENKO (1283–c.1351), JAPAN

442 **Comfort zone** "Minds, like bodies, will often fall into a pimpled, ill-conditioned state from mere excess of comfort."
CHARLES DICKENS (1812–1870), ENGLAND

443 **DO AS YOU WILL**
As a maxim for how to live, "Do as you will" sounds like a recipe for mayhem. No one would say it to a roomful of schoolchildren. But it can be wise advice, for it appeals to the inherent wisdom in all of us. Like diners in an "all you can eat" restaurant, we would soon find that too much is a bad thing, and we set our own limits when they have not been set for us.

444 **Taoist advice** "Know contentment and no disgrace will befall you. Know when to stop and you will encounter no danger."
LAOZI (6TH CENTURY BC), CHINA

Finding Fulfilment

445 SEIZING TODAY AND TOMORROW
"Even while we speak," wrote Horace more than two millennia ago, "envious time has passed. Seize the day [*carpe diem*], putting as little trust as possible in tomorrow!" But we can seize the day without relinquishing trust in our ambitions. It's a question of taking action – not only to enjoy the present but also to build for the future. If we don't look forward with hope, then there may come a time when we have cause to look back with regret.

---

446 Precious time "Not one single moment of life can be regained for millions of gold coins. Therefore, what greater loss is there than time spent fruitlessly?"
CHANAKYA PANDITA (350–275 BC), INDIA

447 Memento mori "We should always be mindful of the ever-present prospect of death, and never forget it for an instant.

If we do so, the distractions of the world will not infect us
and it will be easier for us to follow our path in earnest."
YOSHIDA KENKO (1283–c.1351), JAPAN

448 **Maximum impact** "Life is a series of collisions with the
future; it is not the sum of what we have been, but what
we yearn to be."
JOSÉ ORTEGA Y GASSET (1883–1955), SPAIN

449 **Step one; step two** "First tell yourself what you want to be;
and then do what you need to do."
EPICTETUS (55–c.135), GREECE

---

450 **BECAUSE IT'S THERE**
Ancient peoples thought of mountain-tops
as the inaccessible abode of gods and spirits.
By the nineteenth century, the majesty of
mountain scenery became an inspiration and
an irresistible challenge, which was summed

up by the British mountaineer George Mallory (1886–1924) who, asked why men should want to scale Mount Everest, replied, "Because it's there." We all have our personal Everests: it's up to us whether to climb them or to walk around them.

---

451 The summit of ambition "Never measure the height of a mountain until you have reached the top. Then you will see how low it was."
DAG HAMMARSKJÖLD
(1905–1961), SWEDEN

452 Simple advice
"Love, and do as you will."
ST AUGUSTINE OF HIPPO
(354–430), NORTH AFRICA

453 **Our true life** "We must remind ourselves as often as possible that our true life is not this external, material life that passes before our eyes here on Earth, but that it is the inner life of our spirit for which the visible life serves only as a scaffolding – a necessary aid to our spiritual growth … We must remind ourselves and one another that the scaffolding has no meaning or importance, except to make possible the erection of the building itself."

LEO TOLSTOY (1828–1910), RUSSIA

454 **Making waves** "A great revolution in just one individual will help to change the destiny of all humankind."

DAISAKU IKEDA (BORN 1928), JAPAN

455 **An unstoppable force** "The Path is like getting onto a train that you cannot get off. You roll on and on."

CHÖGYAM TRUNGPA RINPOCHE (1939–1987), TIBET

456 **Keep going** "The best way out is always through."

ROBERT FROST (1874–1963), USA

457 **One step beyond** "By attempting the impossible one can attain the highest level of the possible."
AUGUST STRINDBERG (1849–1912), SWEDEN

458 **Ask questions later** "Life can only be understood backwards: but it must be lived forwards."
SØREN KIERKEGAARD (1813–1855), DENMARK

459 **Considered response** "One's action ought to come out of an achieved stillness: not to be a mere rushing on."
D.H. LAWRENCE (1885–1930), ENGLAND

---

460 **SELF-ACTUALIZATION**
The twentieth-century American psychologist Abraham Maslow developed the concept of the hierarchy of needs. He believed that the satisfaction of one requirement led seamlessly to awareness of the next: when

we are hungry we prioritize eating, but once we have eaten we may think about more advanced needs, such as security, love and esteem. Beyond all these is the desire for self-actualization – the sense that we have realized our full potential.

---

461   **Be what you can** "A musician must make music, an artist must paint, a poet must write, if he is to be at peace with himself. What a man can be, he must be."
ABRAHAM MASLOW (1908–1970), USA

462   **A true course** "Our plans fail because they have no aim. For the sailor who does not know where to set his course, there are no favourable winds."
SENECA (4 BC–AD 65), ROME

463 **A welcome by-product** "Success usually comes to those who are too busy to be looking for it."

HENRY DAVID THOREAU (1817–1862), USA

464 **The time is now** "If you postpone spiritual practice until you have gained all your worldly ambitions, you will never have time for spiritual practice."

YOSHIDA KENKO (1283–c.1351), JAPAN

465 **A distant prospect** "Far away there in the sunshine are my highest aspirations. I may not reach them, but I can look up and see their beauty, believe in them, and try to follow where they lead."

LOUISA MAY ALCOTT (1832–1888), USA

---

466 **THE DREAM OF ULYSSES**
Travel is an inexhaustible source of wisdom. We learn not only about new places, but also about ourselves – our ability to adapt to

different customs and meet new challenges. This stimulation is hard to give up. Even Ulysses, the archetypal adventurer, still longs in old age for one last journey, "To follow knowledge like a sinking star, Beyond the utmost bound of human thought" (from "Ulysses" by Alfred Lord Tennyson).

---

467 **The path of eternity** "The endless road is the only one worth travelling."

MODERN SUFIC SAYING

468 **Full circle** "For enlightenment to happen the perceiver must turn right around and wake up to the fact that he is face to face with his own nature – that HE IS IT. The spiritual seeker ultimately finds that he was already at the destination, that he himself IS what he had been seeking and he was in fact already home."

RAMESH S. BALSEKAR (BORN 1917), INDIA

HAPPINESS

469 **Perfect concord** "Happiness is when what you think, what you say, and what you do are in harmony."
MAHATMA GANDHI (1869–1948), INDIA

470 **Unquenchable thirsts** "He who loves money will not be satisfied with money; nor he who loves wealth, with gain: this also is vanity."
ECCLESIASTES 5.10

471 **Butterflies** "Happiness is like a butterfly which, when pursued, is always beyond our grasp, but, if you will sit down quietly, may alight upon you."
NATHANIEL HAWTHORNE (1804–1864), USA

472 **COUNT YOUR BLESSINGS**
The Shawnee chief, Tecumseh, once said: "If you see nothing to be thankful for, be certain that it is your own fault." When we're constantly looking out for the next pleasure,

the next acquisition, the next career goal, we can overlook the positive things that are right in front of our eyes. It's important to remind ourselves of our blessings. Living in a state of endless gratitude is more rewarding than living in a state of restless dissatisfaction.

---

473 **Be thankful** "Remember that what you have now was once among the things you only hoped for."
EPICURUS (c.341–270 BC), GREECE

474 **Job satisfaction** "Pleasure in the task puts perfection in the work."
ARISTOTLE (384–322 BC), GREECE

475 **Everyday happiness** "One ought, every day at least, to hear a little song, read a good poem, see a fine picture, and if it were possible, to speak a few reasonable words."
JOHANN WOLFGANG VON GOETHE (1749–1832), GERMANY

476   **Time and culture** "There can be no high civilization where there is not ample leisure."

HENRY WARD BEECHER (1813–1887), USA

---

477   **WORK AND LEISURE**
In antiquity work was seen as a divine curse to punish man's disobedience. The Greek for work was *ponos*, which meant sorrow. In the sixteenth century the work ethic arose: all men must work to reshape the world as the Kingdom of God. The secular version valued diligence, punctuality, deferment of gratification. But to humanize the workplace it was necessary to concede holidays. And in modern times the idea of time to oneself, for the nurture of the soul, has acquired a new sacredness. Some people would say that the work ethic is destructive; while others find in work a counterweight to family life.

478 **The thrill of the chase** "Everyone needs to work.
Even a lion cannot sleep, expecting a deer to enter
his mouth."

HITOPADESHA (14TH CENTURY), INDIA

479 **Work, then play** "We forgo leisure in order that we may
acquire leisure, just as some go to war in order that they
may have peace."

ARISTOTLE (384–322 BC), GREECE

480 **Don't worry, be happy** "Happiness cannot be found in great effort and willpower, but it is already there in relaxation and letting go."
LAMA GENDUN RINPOCHE (1918–1997), TIBET

481 **Simple pleasures** "That man is the richest whose pleasures are the cheapest."
HENRY DAVID THOREAU (1817–1862), USA

482 **Excess baggage** "There is no heavier burden than having too many desires."
LAOZI (6TH CENTURY BC), CHINA

483 **THE WAY OF LAUGHTER**
In medieval monasteries, laughter was forbidden: it was seen as too close to hysteria, dangerously over-exciting. Today, we have a better understanding of laughter in its many forms, and we know how

therapeutic and cathartic it can be. Wisdom is still often associated with seriousness and even solemnity, but we no longer associate laughter with foolishness or insanity. And smiles are intriguingly ambivalent: we smile when we're amused and we smile when we're happy. Does this point to a profound link between laughter and contentment?

484   **Defenceless** "Against the assault of laughter nothing can stand."
MARK TWAIN (1835–1910), USA

485   **Eat well, be well** "The discovery of a new recipe does more for human happiness than the discovery of a star."
ANTHELME BRILLAT-SAVARIN (1755–1826), FRANCE

486   **Spontaneity** "I am not here to think, but to be, feel, live!"
JOHANN GOTTFRIED HERDER (1744–1803), GERMANY

487   THE CONSOLATION OF PHILOSOPHY
"In every turn of ill-fortune the most unfortunate man is the one who once was happy," wrote Boethius (c.480–524), one of the last great men of Rome before the Dark Ages. Condemned to death by the Gothic ruler Theodoric, he wrote *The Consolation of Philosophy*, drawing on all his knowledge and insight to show how even in affliction the soul can recognize and reach out to the ideal of goodness and the ultimate reality of God. The true happiness of a virtuous mind is its ability to commune with God. Countless people since have found comfort and encouragement in Boethius's wisdom.

---

488   A duty to ourselves "There is no duty which we so much underrate as that of being happy."
ROBERT LOUIS STEVENSON (1850–1894), SCOTLAND

489 **Life is there to be enjoyed** "All animals, except man, know that the principal business of life is to enjoy it."
SAMUEL BUTLER (1835–1902), ENGLAND

490 **A sunny spirit** "Humour is the great thing, the saving thing. The minute it crops up, all our irritations and resentments slip away, and a sunny spirit takes their place."
MARK TWAIN (1835–1910), USA

491 **Chasing rainbows** "Virtue is its own reward, and brings with it the truest and highest pleasure; but if we cultivate it only for pleasure's sake, we are selfish, not religious, and will never gain the pleasure, because we can never have the virtue."
JOHN HENRY NEWMAN (1801–1890), ENGLAND

492 **Obstacles to success** "Six foibles need to be overcome in order to achieve success: drowsiness, indolence, fear, anger, slovenliness and verbosity."
ANCIENT SANSKRIT VERSE

493 **Keep it simple** "Greater happiness comes with simplicity than with complexity."
THE BUDDHA (c.563–c.483 BC), INDIA

494 **Two steps away** "Happiness, it seems to me, consists of two things: first, in being where you belong, and second – and best – in comfortably going through everyday life, that is, having had a good night's sleep and not being hurt by new shoes."
THEODOR FONTANE (1819–1898), GERMANY

495 **As old as you feel** "It is better to be seventy years young than forty years old."
OLIVER WENDELL HOLMES (1809–1894), USA

496 **In a mellow tone** "Age is not all decay: it is the ripening, the swelling, of the fresh life within, that withers and bursts the husk."
GEORGE MACDONALD (1824–1905), SCOTLAND

497   **No turning back** "No mirror ever became iron again. No bread ever became wheat; no ripened grape ever became sour fruit. Mature yourself and be secure from a change for the worse. Become the light."
JALAL AD-DIN RUMI (1207–1273), PERSIA

498   **Defy analysis** "Ask yourself whether you are happy and you cease to be so."
JOHN STUART MILL (1806–1873), ENGLAND

499   **Essential ingredient** "Dost thou love life? Then do not squander time, for that is the stuff life is made of."
BENJAMIN FRANKLIN (1706–1790), USA

500   **Feelgood factors** "The best doctors in the world are Doctor Diet, Doctor Quiet, and Doctor Merryman."
JONATHAN SWIFT (1667–1745), IRELAND

501   **Anticipation** "Pleasure disappoints: possibility never."
SØREN KIERKEGAARD (1813–1855), DENMARK

502 **Mountaineering** "There are many paths up the mountain, but the view of the moon from the top is the same."
ANCIENT JAPANESE SAYING

503 **Blessed are the careful** "It is from care that blessings arise. It is from carelessness that troubles arise."
THE BUDDHA (c.563–c.483 BC), INDIA

504 **No small matter** "Be satisfied with success in even the smallest matter. And think that even such a result is no trifle."
MARCUS AURELIUS (121–180), ROME

505 **Intrinsic benefit** "The reward of a thing well done is to have done it."
RALPH WALDO EMERSON (1803–1882), USA

506 **Elementary algebra** "If A is success in life, then A equals x plus y plus z. Work is x; y is play; and z is keeping your mouth shut."
ALBERT EINSTEIN (1879–1955), GERMANY/USA

VOCATIONS

507 JOY IN WORK
The Indian thinker Sri Ramakrishna said that "God created the world in play." Our own tasks become lighter if we can begin to see them as a joyous and positive act of service – an opportunity for creativity. Play is an affirmation – of faith in the positive possibilities we are given as human beings, of fearlessness in the face of life's ups and downs, and of belief in the availability of contentment.

---

508 Permanent vacation "Choose a job that you love, and you will never have to work a day in your life."
CONFUCIUS (551–479 BC), CHINA

509 Extended youth "A man is not old as long as he is seeking something."
JEAN ROSTAND (1894–1977), FRANCE

510   **Prize for effort** "Far and away the best prize that life offers is the chance to work hard at work worth doing."
THEODORE ROOSEVELT (1858–1919), USA

511   **Shades of regret** "Vocations which we wanted to pursue, but didn't, bleed, like coloured dyes, onto the whole of our existence."
HONORÉ DE BALZAC (1799–1850), FRANCE

512   **Dream-catching** "First, have a definite, clear practical ideal – a goal, an objective. Second, have the necessary means to achieve your goal – wisdom, money, materials, and methods. Third, adjust all your means to that goal. People are goal-seeking animals. Our lives only have meaning if we are reaching out and striving for our goals."
ARISTOTLE (384–322 BC), GREECE

513 RENAISSANCE MAN
Before the Renaissance, most Western
societies had some variant on the proverb,
"Let the cobbler stick to his last," and sons
were expected to follow the trade of their
father. One of the liberating effects of the
Renaissance was to show that one man could
be a naturalist, engineer and painter, as
Leonardo was; another, a poet and sculptor,
as Michelangelo was. The achievements of
these so-called Renaissance Men showed
others that there were no summits, artistic or
intellectual, to which one could not climb.

---

514 Everything is possible "It is a world of startling possibilities."
CHARLES FLETCHER DOLE (1845–1927), USA

515 A contrary view "The man who promises everything is sure
to fulfil nothing, and everyone who promises too much is in

danger of using evil means to carry out his promises, and is already on the way to perdition."

CARL GUSTAV JUNG (1875–1961), SWITZERLAND

516 **Spread your wings** "One can never consent to creep when one feels an impulse to soar."

HELEN KELLER (1880–1968), USA

517 **Starting with self** "You must be the change you wish to see in the world."

MAHATMA GANDHI (1869–1948), INDIA

518 **We are what we do** "What we think, or what we know, or what we believe in, is, in the end, of little consequence. The only consequence is what we do."

JOHN RUSKIN (1819–1900), ENGLAND

519 **Secret ingredient** "Let me tell you the secret that has led me to my goal. My strength lies solely in my tenacity."

LOUIS PASTEUR (1822–1895), FRANCE

520 **Your future** "Stand up, be bold, be strong. Take the whole responsibility on your own shoulders, and know that you are the creator of your own destiny. All the strength and succour you want is within you. Therefore, make your own future."
SWAMI VIVEKANANDA (1863–1902), INDIA

521 **Chain reaction** "One thing life has taught me: if you are interested, you never have to look for new interests. They come to you. When you are genuinely interested in one thing, it will always lead to something else."
ELEANOR ROOSEVELT (1884–1962), USA

522 **Music lessons** "Life is like playing a violin in public and learning the instrument as one goes along."
SAMUEL BUTLER (1835–1902), ENGLAND

523 **Eloquent action** "I think one's feelings waste themselves in words, they ought all to be distilled into actions and into actions which bring results."
FLORENCE NIGHTINGALE (1820–1910), ENGLAND

524 **Eyes forward** "I never see what has been done;
I only see what remains to be done."
MARIE CURIE (1867–1934), POLAND

525 **Feed your ambitions** "To be always intending to live a new
life, but never find time to set about it – this is as if a man
should put off eating and drinking from one day to another
till he be starved and destroyed."
WALTER SCOTT (1771–1832), SCOTLAND

526 **PRIORITY CHECK**
Rabbi Mendel Epstein has said: "If you are
too busy to spend time with your children,
then you are busier than God intended you
to be." Our time is a precious and finite
resource, under constant pressure from a
multitude of concerns. Whenever we spend
time doing something, we deny ourselves
the opportunity to do something else, and

so we need to weigh up whether the cost of this lost opportunity is worth bearing. This fundamental economic principle, known as "opportunity cost", is just as valid in the micro-economies of our lives as in the world of commerce.

---

527 **Fool's gold** "Gold dust is precious, but when it gets in your eyes, it blurs your vision."
XITANG (735–814), CHINA

528 **Against complacency** "Nothing wilts faster than laurels that have been rested upon."
PERCY BYSSHE SHELLEY (1792–1822), ENGLAND

529 **Go all the way** "If you must begin, then go all the way, because if you begin and quit, the unfinished business you have left behind will haunt you for all time."
CHÖGYAM TRUNGPA RINPOCHE (1939–1987), TIBET

CREATIVITY

530 **Speak your mind** "Originality does not consist in saying what no one has ever said before, but in saying exactly what you think yourself."

JAMES STEPHENS (1882–1950), IRELAND

531 **Object lesson** "It's not what you look at that matters, it's what you see."

HENRY DAVID THOREAU (1817–1862), USA

532 **Liberation** "I saw the angel in the marble and carved until I set him free."

MICHELANGELO BUONARROTI (1475–1564), ITALY

533 **The beginning of the end** "To fall into a habit is to begin to cease to be."

MIGUEL DE UNAMUNO (1864–1936), SPAIN

534 **A leap into the unknown** "Creativity requires the courage to let go of certainties."

ERICH FROMM (1900–1980), GERMANY/USA

535   **A happy discovery** "An artist is someone who turns his coat inside out and falls in love with the colour of the lining."
JEANNE TARDIVEAU (BORN 1963), FRANCE

536   **One after the other** "Inspiration follows aspiration."
RABINDRANATH TAGORE (1861–1941), INDIA

537   **Demystification** "All you have to do is touch the right key at the right time, and the instrument will play itself."
JOHANN SEBASTIAN BACH (1685–1750), GERMANY

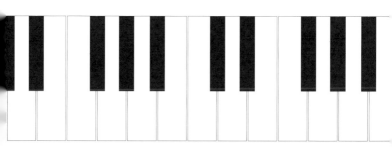

538 **The next step** "If you can walk you can dance. If you can speak you can sing."
ZIMBABWEAN PROVERB

539 **Focal point** "Concentrate all your thoughts on the task in hand. The sun's rays do not burn until brought to a focus."
ALEXANDER GRAHAM BELL (1847–1922), SCOTLAND/USA

540 **The creative spark** "The possible's slow fuse is lit by the imagination."
EMILY DICKINSON (1830–1886), USA

541 **Daydreamers** "They who dream by day are cognizant of many things which escape those who dream only by night."
EDGAR ALLAN POE (1809–1849), USA

542 **Achieving the impossible** "The difficult is what takes a little time: the impossible is what takes a little longer."
FRIDTJOF NANSEN (1861–1930), NORWAY

543   **A BRIGHT TOOL OF THOUGHT**
Metaphor is a way of thinking which imaginatively transfers qualities of one thing to something else, to which they are not literally applicable. It was once memorably – and metaphorically – described as a tool left behind by God in the race of beings – humanity – which He had created. As a form of expression that transcends basic description, it is one of the great conduits of wisdom. The wise value metaphor as a fisherman values his nets.

---

544   **Experienced wisdom** "All truly wise thoughts have been thought already thousands of times; but to make them truly ours, we must think them over again honestly, till they take root in our personal experience."

JOHANN WOLFGANG VON GOETHE (1749–1832), GERMANY

Lighting
the Dark

PERCEPTION AND
UNDERSTANDING

545   **The long view** "If the doors of perception were cleansed everything would appear to man as it is, infinite."

WILLIAM BLAKE (1757–1827), ENGLAND

---

546   **DHYANA**

For Buddhists and Hindus, the key to stilling the "monkey of the mind" is the practice of sitting silently in meditation, or *dhyana*. The aim is a transformation of consciousness, bringing us to a state of awareness that allows us to penetrate the surface of our habitual thoughts and beliefs to perceive the world as it really is.

---

547   **Limitless comprehension** "Stop talking, stop thinking, and there is nothing you will not understand."

JIANZHI SENGCAN (KANCHI SOSAN) (DIED 606), CHINA

548 **Perceiving the divine** "Eyes cannot see the supreme being nor can words express it – nor can it be perceived by other senses and cognitive faculties. The supreme being is revealed only in meditation. Meditation is possible only when consciousness becomes purified by knowledge of the self."
UPANISHADS (c.600 BC)

549 **Attuned to the miraculous** "Miracles ... seem to me to rest not so much on faces or voices or healing power coming suddenly near to us from afar off, but upon our perceptions being made finer, so that for a moment our eyes can see and our ears can hear what there is about us always."
WILLA CATHER (1873–1947), USA

550 **When a thief sees a saint ...** "Whatever we perceive in the world around us reflects who we are and what we care about most deeply, as in the old saying, 'When a thief sees a saint, all he sees are his pockets.'"
ROBERT FRAGER (BORN 1940), USA

551   **THE LIMITATIONS OF LANGUAGE**
Have you ever tried to think without using words? The effort required shows our immense dependence on language. Our relationship with language has occupied numerous twentieth-century philosophers, such as Ludwig Wittgenstein and Gilbert Ryle. The vocabulary and structure of our speech confine, as well as express, our thoughts. Language channels our perception between its invisible walls.

---

552   **Outer edges** "The limits of my language are the limits of my world."

LUDWIG WITTGENSTEIN (1889–1951), AUSTRIA/ENGLAND

553   **Constant craving** "We have a hunger of the mind which asks for knowledge of all around us, and the more we gain, the more is our desire; the more we see, the more we are capable of seeing."

MARIA MITCHELL (1818–1889), USA

554 **Heart to heart** "If words come out of the heart, they will enter the heart, but if they come from the tongue, they will not pass beyond the ears."

AL-SUHRAWARDI (1154–1191), PERSIA

555 **Sensory perception**

"The eye of the silent heart will see into great depths, and the ear of the silent mind will hear untold wonders."

ST HESYCHIUS OF JERUSALEM (5TH CENTURY)

556 HOW DOES IT FEEL TO BE A BAT?

The philosopher Thomas Nagel published a famous paper in 1974 about what it might be like to be a bat. His aim was to show the impossibility of connecting with another creature's sense of their own being. We might be extremely knowledgeable about bat brains, but the experience of the bat is unavailable to us. Subjective experience – that is, consciousness – will always be deeply mysterious, and this is true of our fellow humans as well as other species. Actual experience cannot be transmitted to another person. And even within ourselves an experience changes over time: when recalled, it is no longer itself but something recreated.

557 **Listening for what cannot be heard** "The reality of the other person lies not in what he reveals to you, but what he cannot reveal to you. Therefore, if you would understand him, listen not to what he says, but rather to what he does not say."

KAHLIL GIBRAN (1883–1931), LEBANON/USA

558 **Limited view** "It is one of the commonest of mistakes to consider that the limit of our power of perception is also the limit of all there is to perceive."

CHARLES WEBSTER LEADBEATER (1847–1934), ENGLAND

559 **THE TRIPLE SELF**
The ancient Greeks divided the soul into three parts: desiring, spirited and reasoning. Many centuries later, Sigmund Freud echoed this notion by suggesting that the self was divided into three: Ego, Superego and Id. The Ego is our thinking mind, our sense of

being who we are. The Superego and the Id are unthinking: the Id holds our most basic urges for gratification while the Superego acts as our conscience and keeps the Id in check. Whether these interpretations are accurate or not, they have equipped psychologists with ways of coming to terms with not only our conscious minds, but also our dreams and deepest desires.

---

560 **Refining our vision** "The history of the living world can be summarized as the elaboration of ever more perfect eyes within a cosmos in which there is always something more to be seen."

PIERRE TEILHARD DE CHARDIN (1881–1955), FRANCE

561 **Strength or weakness?** "Many a man fails to become a thinker only for the reason that his memory is too good."

FRIEDRICH WILHELM NIETZSCHE (1844–1900), GERMANY

562 **Instinct and reason** "All our progress is an unfolding, like a vegetable bud. You have first an instinct, then an opinion, then a knowledge as the plant has root, bud, and fruit. Trust the instinct to the end, though you can render no reason."
RALPH WALDO EMERSON (1803–1882), USA

563 **The difficulty of thinking well** "As nothing is more easy than to think, so nothing is more difficult than to think well. The easiness of thinking we received from God; the difficulty of thinking well proceeded from ourselves."
THOMAS TRAHERNE (C.1637–1674), ENGLAND

564 **The great lever** "Mind is the great lever of all things; human thought is the process by which human ends are ultimately answered."
DANIEL WEBSTER (1782–1852), USA

565 **Beyond the horizon** "They are ill discoverers that think there is no land, when they can see nothing but sea."
FRANCIS BACON (1561–1626), ENGLAND

WISDOM AND EXPERIENCE

566   **WHAT DO I KNOW?**
"Que sais-je?" ("What do I know?") was the motto of Michel de Montaigne, the sixteenth-century French essayist whose amiable good sense still endears him to many readers today. His question was intended to remind him that knowledge was there to be tested and tried. But it was also a reminder that he, an educated and quite wealthy man, well-read and with his own library of books, actually knew very little.

---

567   **Natural instinct** "All men by their nature desire knowledge."
ARISTOTLE (384–322 BC), GREECE

568   **Beyond knowledge** "Knowledge is merely brilliance in the organization of ideas. It is not true wisdom. The truly wise go beyond knowledge."
CONFUCIUS (551–479 BC), CHINA

569 **Due consideration** "Do not learn how to react,
but how to respond."
THE BUDDHA (c.563–c.483 BC), INDIA

570 **Sometime never** "What may be done at any time
will be done at no time."
SCOTTISH PROVERB

571 **Rich and poor** "Poverty does not bring wisdom,
but wisdom inescapably brings poverty."
ANCIENT SANSKRIT VERSE, INDIA

572 **Keep your counsel** "Those who have knowledge do not
speak. Those who speak do not have knowledge."
LAOZI (6TH CENTURY BC), CHINA

573 **Practical wisdom** "There is no good in arguing with the
inevitable. The only argument available with an east wind
is to put on your overcoat."
JAMES RUSSELL LOWELL (1819–1891), USA

574 **Pride of learning** "The ignorant are speedily convinced, and the wise are soon persuaded by argument. But all the wisdom in heaven has a hard task to overcome the pride of an obstinate scholar."

ANCIENT SANSKRIT VERSE, INDIA

575 **One thing in common** "Only the wisest and the least wise never change."

CONFUCIUS (551–479 BC), CHINA

576 **Top heavy** "Power without wisdom collapses under its own weight."

HORACE (65–8 BC), ROME

577 **GIFTS OF THE HOLY SPIRIT**
Seven gifts of the Holy Spirit are listed in St Jerome's version of the Bible, the Vulgate (Isaiah, 11.2). They are: wisdom, understanding, counsel, fortitude, knowledge, piety,

and fear of the Lord. The truly wise person does not only know the things of God but experiences and lives them. By acquiring wisdom through experience, the other six gifts follow naturally.

---

578 **A head start** "Dare to be wise: when you begin you are already halfway there."
HORACE (65–8 BC), ROME

579 **Everyday insight** "There is no enlightenment outside of daily life."
THICH NHAT HANH (BORN 1926), VIETNAM/FRANCE

580 **Made to measure** "The perfection of wisdom, and the end of true philosophy is to proportion our wants to our possessions, our ambitions to our capacities, we will then be a happy and a virtuous people."
MARK TWAIN (1835–1910), USA

581 **Time for reflection** "Let your mind become clear like a still woodland pond."

THE BUDDHA (c.563–c.483 BC), INDIA

582 **True parent** "Memory is the mother of all wisdom."

AESCHYLUS (525–456 BC), GREECE

583 **Insect wisdom** "The men of experiment are like the ant, they only collect and use; the reasoners resemble spiders, who make cobwebs out of their own substance. But the bee takes the middle course: it gathers its material from the flowers of the garden and field, but transforms and digests it by a power of its own."
FRANCIS BACON (1561–1626), ENGLAND

584 **All-encompassing** "To the wise, nothing is alien or remote."
ANTISTHENES (C.444–C.370 BC), GREECE

585 **Line of succession** "At 20 years of age the will reigns, at 30 the wit, at 40 the judgment."
BENJAMIN FRANKLIN (1706–1790), USA

586 **Self-taught** "Axioms in philosophy are not axioms until they are proved upon our pulses: we read fine things but never feel them to the full until we have gone the same steps as the author."
JOHN KEATS (1795–1821), ENGLAND

587 **Inner wealth** "What is stored within is greater than oil, and it satisfies our appetites more than meat. It is joy to the heart, light to the eye, speed to the foot, and shield to the breast."

KEBRA NAGAST (C.13TH CENTURY), ETHIOPIA

---

588 **LEADERSHIP**
For the Taoist, a leader is best when people barely know that he or she is there. Laozi, the ancient Chinese philosopher commonly regarded as the founder of Taoism, gave this prescription for good government: "To lead the people, walk behind them."

---

589 **All their own work?** "Of a good leader, when his work is done the people will say, 'We did this ourselves.'"

LAOZI (6TH CENTURY BC), CHINA

590 **Captured wisdom** "Wise men learn many things from their enemies."
ARISTOPHANES (448–380 BC), GREECE

591 **Grooming** "Experience is a comb which nature gives us when we are bald."
BELGIAN PROVERB

592 **Razor sharp** "Sages say that the path of wisdom is narrow and difficult to tread, as narrow as the edge of a razor."
UPANISHADS (C.600 BC)

593 **THE CATEGORICAL IMPERATIVE**
Ethics examines the question, How should we live? One answer given by Immanuel Kant (1724–1804) involves the Categorical Imperative – the belief that everyone should follow only those principles that they would like to see applied universally. Immorality

occurs when people set special standards for themselves alone.

---

594   **A difficult ascent** "All rising to a great place is by a winding stair."
FRANCIS BACON (1561–1626), ENGLAND

595   **People's bank** "Common experience is the gold reserve which confers an exchange value on the currency of our words; without this reserve of shared experiences, all our pronouncements are cheques drawn on insufficient funds."
RENÉ DAUMAL (1908–1944), FRANCE

---

596   **SADDER AND WISER?**
In Samuel Taylor Coleridge's poem *The Rime of the Ancient Mariner*, the man who hears the mariner's tale of sorrow is deeply affected: "A sadder and a wiser man, He rose the

morrow morn." But can a person also be *happier* and wiser? It is easier, it seems, to learn from painful experience than from pleasure. The burnt child fears the fire, but the unburnt child knows only that the fire is pleasantly warm.

---

597   **A barbed comment** "One thorn of experience is worth a whole wilderness of warning."
JAMES RUSSELL LOWELL (1819–1891), USA

598   **Path of least resistance** "Don't break your shin on a stool that is not in your way."
IRISH PROVERB

599   **More questions than answers** "A great philosophy is not one that passes final judgments and establishes ultimate truth. It is one that causes uneasiness and starts commotion."
CHARLES PÉGUY (1873–1914), FRANCE

600 **The art of elimination** "In the mind of the beginner there are many possibilities. In the mind of the expert there are few."
THE BUDDHA (c.563–c.483 BC), INDIA

601 **A simple solution** "It is impossible to walk rapidly and be unhappy."
MOTHER TERESA (1910–1997), MACEDONIA/INDIA

602 **The chicken and the egg** "A hen is only an egg's way of making another egg."
SAMUEL BUTLER (1835–1902), ENGLAND

603 **Two wrongs** "To overcome evil with good is good; to overcome evil with evil is evil."
MUHAMMAD (570–632)

604 **THE WISDOM OF PARADOX**
The seeming absurdity of a paradox – a statement whose terms apparently contradict

each other – may carry a valuable insight. Often it is a provocative thought, meant to shock a little, as in this example from the English writer G.K. Chesterton: "To be clever enough to get all that money, one must be stupid enough to want it."

---

605 **Radical action** "Men of most renowned virtue have sometimes by transgressing most truly kept the law."
JOHN MILTON (1608–1674), ENGLAND

606 **An unsustainable loss** "If you took all the experience and judgment of people over fifty out of the world, there wouldn't be enough left to run it."
HENRY FORD (1863–1947), USA

607 **Delayed gratification** "Burdens are the foundations of ease and bitter things the forerunners of pleasure."
JALAL AD-DIN RUMI (1207–1273), PERSIA

608 **Treasure hunt** "Wisdom is often nearer when we stoop than when we soar."
WILLIAM WORDSWORTH (1770–1850), ENGLAND

609 **A discerning mind** "It is a sign of an educated mind to be able to entertain a thought without accepting it."
ARISTOTLE (384–322 BC), GREECE

610 **Salient points** "To understand reality is not the same as to know about outward events. It is to perceive the essential nature of things. The best-informed man is not necessarily the wisest. Indeed there is a danger that precisely in the multiplicity of his knowledge he will lose sight of what is essential. But on the other hand, knowledge of an apparently trivial detail quite often makes it possible to see into the depth of things. And so the wise man will seek to acquire the best possible knowledge about events, but always without becoming dependent upon this knowledge. To recognize the significant in the factual is wisdom."
DIETRICH BONHOEFFER (1906–1945), GERMANY

611   **Learning on the job** "For the things we have to learn before we can do them, we learn by doing them."
HANNAH ARENDT (1906–1975), GERMANY/USA

612   **A design for life** "Science is organized knowledge. Wisdom is organized life."
IMMANUEL KANT (1724–1804), GERMANY

613   **False economy** "There is no economy in going to bed early to save candles if the result be twins."
CHINESE PROVERB

614   **Protective coating** "What strikes the oyster does not damage the pearl."
JALAL AD-DIN RUMI (1207–1273), PERSIA

615   **A quality of grace** "Grace must find expression in life, otherwise it is not grace."
KARL BARTH (1886–1968), SWITZERLAND

616 **Better informed** "The man who reads nothing at all
is better educated than the man who reads nothing
but newspapers."

THOMAS JEFFERSON (1743–1826), USA

617 **Miniature fable** "A donkey with a load of holy books is still a donkey."
TRADITIONAL SUFI SAYING

618 **By degrees** "Enlightenment must come little by little – otherwise it would overwhelm."
IDRIES SHAH (1924–1996), AFGHANISTAN

619 **Priorities** "Besides the noble art of getting things done, there is the noble art of leaving things undone. The wisdom of life consists in the elimination of non-essentials."
LIN YUTANG (1895–1976), CHINA

620 **Untapped potential** "Genius without education is like silver in the mine."
BENJAMIN FRANKLIN (1706–1790), USA

621 **Self-confidence** "As soon as you trust yourself, you will know how to live."
JOHANN WOLFGANG VON GOETHE (1749–1832), GERMANY

622 **Light and shade** "We could never learn to be brave and patient if there were only joy in the world."
HELEN KELLER
(1880–1968), USA

623 **Personal morality** "A wise person, even though all laws were abolished, would still lead the same life."
ARISTOPHANES
(448–380 BC), GREECE

624 **Words of experience** "How vain it is to sit down to write when you have not stood up to live."
HENRY DAVID THOREAU
(1817–1862), USA

TEACHERS AND SAGES

625 **THE GURU**
Buddhists and Hindus lay great emphasis on finding the best teacher, or *guru*, to guide the seeker after wisdom and insight. It may take some time to discover the ideal person from whom to learn. A true *guru* should be able to attune perfectly – and empathetically – to our needs and abilities.

---

626 **Flying school** "To find the *guru* is a great boon: without him, we are lost, like a moth that is attracted by the lamp and falls into the flame. Delusion is the lamp, we are the moth flying around the flame. We fall. But thanks to the wisdom of the guru, some of us are saved."
KABIR (1440–1518), INDIA

627 **The teacher's true path** "The sage shuns excess, extravagance, and arrogance."
LAOZI (6TH CENTURY BC), CHINA

628 Head of the class "The teacher should have maximal
authority and minimal power."

THOMAS SZÁSZ (BORN 1920), HUNGARY/USA

629 Knowing and understanding "When I desire to know, I
seek out the man of learning. When I desire to understand,
I seek out the man of wisdom."

MAHMUD IBN TELI (15TH CENTURY), IRAQ

630 Fragrant wisdom "Hold on firmly to good friends and
fine teachers. Riches and power are fleeting dreams, but
the fragrance of wise words lingers in the world."

HANSHAN (7TH CENTURY), CHINA

---

631 OCCAM'S RAZOR
Many philosophers of the Middle Ages
proposed highly elaborate and fanciful
explanations of metaphysical problems.
However, William of Occam (1285–1349)

wrote a famous dictum that warned against such excesses: "It is vain to do with more what can be done with fewer." This principle became known as "Occam's Razor", since it cuts away all unjustifiable speculation from a hypothesis, leaving the simplest, most plausible explanation.

632 **In praise of simplicity**

"Simplicity is the ultimate sophistication."

LEONARDO DA VINCI (1452–1519), ITALY

633 **Four pillars of learning** "First, rely on the spirit and meaning of the teachings, not on the words; second, rely on the teachings, not on the personality of the teacher; third, rely on real wisdom, not superficial interpretation; and fourth, rely on the essence of your pure wisdom-mind, not on judgmental perceptions."

THE BUDDHA (C.563–C.483 BC), INDIA

634   THE ABSOLUTE IDEA
Dialectics is the method of arriving at philosophical truth by the exchange of logical arguments. Socrates used it, but it is to the German philosopher Georg Hegel that we owe its modern meaning. He saw it as "a productive clash of opposites" – one idea (thesis) gives rise to its opposite (antithesis), and out of their interaction a third idea arises (synthesis). For Hegel the ultimate synthesis was the Absolute Idea, which comprehends all reality.

---

635   Generous assessment "The learner always begins by finding fault, but the scholar sees the positive merit in everything."
GEORG HEGEL (1770–1831), GERMANY

636   Re-education "To teach is to learn twice."
JOSEPH JOUBERT (1754–1824), FRANCE

637 **Tender-hearted** "The heart of the sage is not solid. The sage is as sensitive to the feelings of others as he is to his own."
LAOZI (6TH CENTURY BC), CHINA

638 **Burning intellect** "A mind is a fire to be kindled, not a vessel to be filled."
PLUTARCH (46–120), GREECE

639 **For all weathers** "Education is an ornament in prosperity and a refuge in adversity."
ARISTOTLE (384–322 BC), GREECE

640 **Question and response** "A wise man's question contains half the answer."
IBN GABIROL (SOLOMON BEN JUDAH) (c.1021–c.1058), SPAIN

641 **Curriculum** "Contemplate the workings of this world, listen to the words of the wise, take all that is good as your own. With this as your base, open your own door to truth. Do not overlook the truth that is right before you. Study how water flows in a valley stream, smoothly and freely between the rocks. Also learn from holy books and wise people. Everything – even mountains, rivers, plants, and trees – should be your teacher."

MORIHEI UESHIBA (1883–1969), JAPAN

642 **The way of the sage** "The way of heaven is to nurture but not to harm. The way of the sage is to strive but not to compete."

LAOZI (6TH CENTURY BC), CHINA

643 **Teaching by example** "Preach the Gospel at all times and when necessary use words."

ST FRANCIS OF ASSISI (C.1181–1226), ITALY

CHILDHOOD

644 **A message from God** "Every child comes with the message that God is not yet discouraged of man."
RABINDRANATH TAGORE (1861–1941), INDIA

645 **Parental guidance** "Children need models rather than critics."
JOSEPH JOUBERT (1754–1824), FRANCE

646 **Changing circumstances** "Do not confine your children to your own learning, for they were born in another time."
CHINESE PROVERB

647 **Learning from children** "Adults can learn from very little children, for the hearts of little children are pure. Therefore, the Great Spirit may show to them many things which older people miss."
BLACK ELK (1863–1950),
OGLALA SIOUX NATION

648 **Youthful spirit** "The wildest colts can make the best horses."
PLUTARCH (46–120), GREECE

649 **Telltale actions** "Even children make themselves known
by their acts, by whether what they do is pure and right."
PROVERBS 20.11

650 **Long-term strategy** "There is no finer investment for any
community than putting milk into babies."
WINSTON CHURCHILL (1874–1965), ENGLAND

651 **Sleeping beauty** "There never was a child so lovely but
his mother was glad to get him asleep."
RALPH WALDO EMERSON (1803–1882), USA

652 **Unhindered progress** "If you want to see what children do,
you must stop giving them things."
NORMAN DOUGLAS (1868–1952), SCOTLAND

653 **Invisible presence** "The greatest sign of success for a teacher is to be able to say, 'The children are now working as if I did not exist'."
MARIA MONTESSORI (1870–1952), ITALY

654 **Beauty's lessons** "The most effective kind of education is that a child should play among lovely things."
PLATO (427–347 BC), GREECE

655 **Playing fair** "In the little world in which children have their existence, whosoever brings them up, there is nothing so finely perceived, and so finely felt, as injustice."
CHARLES DICKENS (1812–1870), ENGLAND

656 **A glimpse of the future** "Youth – full of grace, force, fascination! Do you know that Old Age may come after you, with equal grace, force, fascination?"
WALT WHITMAN (1819–1892), USA

657 **Possible confusion** "The first idea that the child must acquire in order to be actively disciplined is that of the difference between good and evil; and the task of the educator lies in seeing that the child does not confuse good with immobility, and evil with action."
MARIA MONTESSORI (1870–1952), ITALY

658 **The learning adventure** "Every time we teach a child something, we prevent him from discovering it for himself.
JEAN PIAGET (1896–1980), SWITZERLAND

659 **THE WISDOM OF CHILDREN**

Children have limited knowledge and experience, but clear vision and lively curiosity, which the concerns of adult life can obscure and diminish. The Danish writer Hans Christian Andersen (1805–1875) illustrated this point in his story *The Emperor's New Clothes*, in which it took a small boy to point out that the emperor's famous and fine new suit was in fact made of nothing at all. The adults attending the emperor dared not speak out what common sense and the evidence of their eyes told them, in case it showed their lack of sophistication.

MAKING MISTAKES _____

660 **Never fear** "The greatest mistake you can make in life
is to be continually fearing you will make one."
ELBERT HUBBARD (1856–1915), USA

661 **Self-improvement** "No man's error becomes his own law,
nor obliges him to persist in it."
THOMAS HOBBES (1588–1679), ENGLAND

662 **The art of making mistakes** "To undertake a genuine
spiritual path is not to avoid difficulties but to learn the
art of making mistakes wakefully, to bring them to the
transformative power of our heart."
JACK KORNFIELD (BORN 1945), USA

663 **LEARNING FROM SETBACKS**
No one who sets out on their ambitions
can expect a continuously upward trajectory.
Even a mountain climber may have to lose
altitude in order to make progress toward

the summit. Winston Churchill once said: "Success is not final. Failure is not fatal. It is the courage to continue that counts."

664 **Hard lessons** "We learn wisdom from failure much more than from success. We often discover what will do by finding out what will not do; and probably he who never made a mistake never made a discovery."
SAMUEL SMILES (1812–1904), SCOTLAND

665 **Advising caution** "Situations are easier to enter than to exit; but it is only common sense to look for the way out before venturing in."
AESOP (620–560 BC), GREECE

666 **Toward certainty** "If a man will begin in certainties he shall end in doubts; but if he will be content to begin in doubts he shall end in certainties."
FRANCIS BACON (1561–1626), ENGLAND

667   **Ideal conditions** "The season of failure is the best time for sowing the seeds of success."
PARAMAHANSA YOGANANDA (1893–1952), INDIA

668   **Prime critics** "Take heed of your opponents, for they are the first to realize your errors."
ANTISTHENES (c.444–c.370 BC), GREECE

669   **Fool's paradise** "The greatest of faults, I should say, is to be conscious of none."
THOMAS CARLYLE (1795–1881), SCOTLAND

670   **CICERO'S VIEW**
The great Roman orator Cicero remarked that "No fair-minded person would accuse another of being unsteady for changing their opinion." We often fear that others will judge us as weak or vacillating if we change how

we feel about something. But being prepared to be genuinely flexible in our views is a sign not of weakness but of strength.

671 **Elasticity** "What is strong and rigid is snapped and laid low. What is flexible and soft will always prevail."

LAOZI (6TH CENTURY BC), CHINA

672 **Fatal delusion** "The true way to be deceived is to think oneself more knowing than others."
FRANÇOIS, DUC DE LA ROCHEFOUCAULD (1613–1680), FRANCE

673 **An unforgivable fault** "For every sin but the killing of time there is forgiveness."
TRADITIONAL SUFI SAYING

674 **Lessons of history** "People will not look forward to posterity who never look backward to their ancestors."
EDMUND BURKE (1729–1797), IRELAND/ENGLAND

675 **Keeping your head down** "To avoid criticism, be nothing, do nothing, say nothing."
ELBERT HUBBARD (1856–1915), USA

676 **A definition** "An expert is a person who has made all the mistakes that can be made in a very narrow field."
NIELS BOHR (1885–1962), DENMARK

677 **Reserve conclusions** "Whenever a theory appears to you as the only possible one, take this as a sign that you have neither understood the theory nor the problem which it was intended to solve."

KARL POPPER (1902–1994), AUSTRIA/ENGLAND

678 **The importance of being silly**
"If people never did silly things, nothing intelligent would ever get done."

LUDWIG WITTGENSTEIN (1889–1951), AUSTRIA

679 **Dare to be ignorant** "Have the courage to be ignorant of a great number of things, in order to avoid the certainty of being ignorant of everything."

SYDNEY SMITH (1771–1845), ENGLAND

680 **A new leaf** "Whatever difficulties you have had in the past, you can make a fresh start today."

THE BUDDHA (c.563–c.483 BC), INDIA

WISDOM OF THE PAST

681 **Irreplaceable** "Every old man that dies is a library that burns"
AMADOU HAMPATE BA (1901–1991), MALI

682 **The toils of history** "Not to know what has happened in
former times is to be always a child. If no use is made of the
toils of the past, the world must remain always in the infancy
of knowledge."
MARCUS TULLIUS CICERO (C.106–43 BC), ROME

683 **THE LESSONS OF MYTH**
We know very little about certain ancient
peoples other than the myths that they have
passed down to us. These magical stories
can often teach us as much as conventional
history. For example, in Celtic mythology
shape-shifting was a means by which wise
men and women transformed themselves
into different entities as varied as a salmon,
a dog, a swordblade, a ray of light and a

grain of wheat. In these metamorphoses the seer took on not only the outer appearances of different aspects of nature but also their inner experiences, and so attained an extraordinary and timeless spiritual insight. Although we are unable to change our physical form in this way, we can enrich our understanding by always trying to see the world through different eyes.

---

684 **All-time great** "Every man of us has all the centuries in him."
LORD MORLEY (1838–1923), ENGLAND

685 **Asylum-seekers** "A country without a memory is a country of madmen."
GEORGE SANTAYANA (1863–1952), SPAIN/USA

686 **A nation's desserts** "People get the history they deserve."
CHARLES DE GAULLE (1890–1970), FRANCE

687 **Slow learners** "What experience and history teach is this – that people and governments have never learned anything from history, nor acted on principles deduced from history."
GEORG HEGEL (1770–1831), GERMANY

688 **All the world's a stage** "Hegel says somewhere that all great events and personalities in world history reappear in one fashion or another. He forgets to add: the first time as tragedy, the second as farce."
KARL MARX (1818–1883), GERMANY

689 **A better future** "The past is necessarily inferior to the future. That is how we wish it to be. How could we acknowledge any merit in our most dangerous enemy: the past, gloomy prevaricator, execrable teacher?"
TOMMASO MARINETTI (1876–1944), ITALY

690 **Seafaring** "The past is a lighthouse, not a harbour."
RUSSIAN SAYING

691   **Action replay** "Whoever wishes to foresee the future must consult the past; for human events ever resemble those of preceding times. This arises from the fact that they are produced by men who ever have been, and ever shall be, animated by the same passions, and thus they necessarily have the same results."

NICCOLÒ MACHIAVELLI (1469–1527), ITALY

692   **The realist** "You can only predict things after they have happened."

EUGÈNE IONESCO (1912–1994), FRANCE

LEARNING FROM OTHERS

693 **A fair exchange** "The good are the teachers of the bad, and the bad are the raw materials of the good."

LAOZI (6TH CENTURY BC), CHINA

---

694 **MIRROR, MIRROR**
Self-knowledge, to be comprehensive, should include awareness of how we are perceived by others. Could it be that the things we do not know about ourselves are the very things that other people know only too well? After this comes another tough question: are we better off not knowing?

---

695 **Three reflections** "In the mirror of bronze, you can see whether you are properly dressed; in the mirror of history, you can see how a nation rises and falls; in the mirror of other people you can see whether you are right or wrong."

EMPEROR TAIZONG (RULED 599–649), CHINA

696 **Sliding scale** "Best is to know all things; good is to listen when you hear what is right; worst is to be ignorant and deaf to the wisdom of another."
HESIOD (8TH CENTURY BC), GREECE

697 **Tailoring yourself** "Eat according to your own tastes and dress according to the taste of others."
BENGALI PROVERB

698 **Good company** "The noble and the good are a joy to see. To be with them brings happiness. If we never encountered fools, we would always be happy!"
THE BUDDHA (C.563–C.483 BC), INDIA

699 **CAPSULES OF THOUGHT**
Has a tune, a phrase or an image ever stuck in your mind as though it had a life of its own? The British scientist Richard Dawkins would call such things *memes*. Dawkins sees

them as a mental version of genes, passing on thoughts as genes do physical qualities. Any proverb or catchphrase – "A stitch in time …" or "Beam me up" – can be a *meme*, as can an urban myth or a piece of folk wisdom. It's an illuminating way of looking at how we pass on knowledge and "culture".

---

700   **From brain to brain** "Just as genes propagate themselves in the gene pool by leaping from body to body via sperms or eggs, so *meme*s propagate themselves in the *meme* pool by leaping from brain to brain."

RICHARD DAWKINS (BORN 1941), ENGLAND

701   **Over-confidence** "It is unwise to be too sure of one's own wisdom. It is healthy to be reminded that the strongest might weaken and the wisest might err."

MAHATMA GANDHI (1869–1948), INDIA

702 **Self-awareness** "They are best off who know that they do not know. They are worst off who claim to know but do not."
LAOZI (6TH CENTURY BC), CHINA

703 **Among teachers** "Think of yourself as if you were the only unenlightened person in the world. Everyone else is your teacher, doing what is right to help you acquire consummate peace of mind, consummate wisdom, consummate compassion."
THE BUDDHA (c.563–c.483 BC), INDIA

704 **Partial knowledge** "It is true that I know very little. But I prefer that little which is my own."
PAUL GAUGUIN (1848–1903), FRANCE

705 **Home truths** "A wise traveller never despises his own country."
WILLIAM HAZLITT (1778–1830), ENGLAND

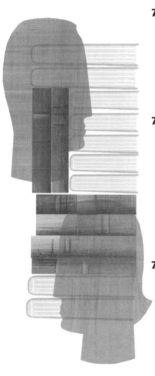

706 Balancing the books

"Beware you be not swallowed up in books! An ounce of love is worth a pound of knowledge."

JOHN WESLEY (1703–1791), ENGLAND

707 Personal tutor

"You have to grow from the inside out. None can teach you, none can make you spiritual. There is no other teacher but your own soul."

SWAMI VIVEKANANDA (1863–1902), INDIA

708 Four wise words

"Teach your tongue to say 'I do not know' and you will make progress."

MAIMONIDES (RABBI MOSES BEN MAIMON) (1135–1204), SPAIN

709   **Working the vein** "When you come to a good book, you must ask yourself: 'Am I inclined to work as an Australian miner would? Are my pickaxes and shovels in good order, and am I in good trim myself, my sleeves well up to the elbow, and my breath good, and my temper?'"
JOHN RUSKIN (1819–1900), ENGLAND

710   **Knowledge and wisdom** "We can be knowledgable with other men's knowledge, but we cannot be wise with other men's wisdom."
MICHEL DE MONTAIGNE (1533–1592), FRANCE

711   **Encounters** "I am defeated, and know it, if I meet any human being from whom I find myself unable to learn anything."
GEORGE HERBERT PALMER (1842–1933), USA

712   **The wisdom of Solomon** "Solomon made a book of proverbs, but a book of proverbs never made a Solomon."
PROVERBIAL SAYING

TESTING TIMES

713 **Problems are good for you** "Man needs difficulties: they are necessary for health."
CARL GUSTAV JUNG (1875–1961), SWITZERLAND

714 **The power of the will** "To succeed, you must have tremendous perseverance, tremendous will. 'I will drink the ocean,' says the persevering soul, 'at my will mountains will crumble up.' Have that sort of energy, that sort of will, work hard, and you will reach your goal."
SWAMI VIVEKANANDA (1863–1902), INDIA

715 **Enjoyment and endurance** "Enjoy when you can, and endure when you must."
JOHANN WOLFGANG VON GOETHE (1749–1832), GERMANY

716 **A talisman** "Courage and perseverance have a magical talisman, before which difficulties disappear and obstacles vanish into air."
JOHN QUINCY ADAMS (1767–1848), USA

717   **Pressed flowers** "Certainly virtue
is like precious odours, most
fragrant when they are incensed,
or crushed: for prosperity doth
best discover vice, but adversity
doth best discover virtue."
FRANCIS BACON (1561–1626), ENGLAND

718   **Moving on** "Finish each day and be done with it.
You have done what you could. Some blunders and
absurdities no doubt crept in; forget them as soon as
you can. Tomorrow is a new day; begin it well and
serenely and with too high a spirit to be cumbered with
your old nonsense."
RALPH WALDO EMERSON (1803–1882), USA

719   **Bouncing back** "Our greatest glory is not in
never falling, but in rising every time we fall."
CONFUCIUS (551–479 BC), CHINA

720 **Foundation stones** "The discipline of suffering, of *great* suffering – do you not know that it is *this* discipline alone that has created every elevation of mankind hitherto?"
FRIEDRICH WILHELM NIETZSCHE (1844–1900), GERMANY

721 **Hardiness** "The little reed, bending with the force of the wind, soon stood upright again when the storm had passed."
AESOP (620–560 BC), GREECE

722 **Clearing the air** "Sorrows gather round great souls as storms do around mountains, but, like them, they break the storm and purify the air of the plain beneath."
JEAN PAUL RICHTER (1763–1825), GERMANY

723 **EMBRACING CHANGE**
In the words of the ancient Greek philosopher Heraclitus, "everything flows and nothing abides, everything yields and nothing

remains permanent". Sometimes it may seem safer to stay where we are than to accept change or take a step into the unknown. But inner peace can only come when we give up worrying about change and trust in life's flow – for the only thing that never changes is change itself.

724   The eternal flow "Some things are rushing into existence, and other things are rushing out of existence; and part of what is now coming into existence has already ceased to exist. Movement and change constantly renew the world, just as the unbroken course of time constantly renews the infinity of the ages. Of all the things that rush by in this flowing stream, in which nothing abides, what is there on which you would set a high price? It would be like falling in love with one of the sparrows in the air when it has already flown out of sight."

MARCUS AURELIUS (121–180), ROME

725 **The person we all need** "Our chief want in life is somebody who shall make us do what we can."
RALPH WALDO EMERSON (1803–1882), USA

726 **Good times, bad times** "What we cultivate in times of ease, we store up to support us in times of change."
THE BUDDHA (c.563–c.483 BC), INDIA

727 **I have lived through this** "You gain strength, courage and confidence by every experience in which you really stop to look fear in the face. You are able to say to yourself, 'I have lived through this horror. I can take the next thing that comes along.'"
ELEANOR ROOSEVELT (1884–1962), USA

728 **The ultimate challenge** "There was never yet philosopher that could endure the toothache patiently."
WILLIAM SHAKESPEARE (1564–1616), ENGLAND

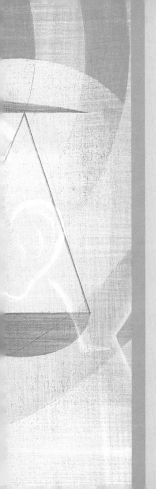

Emotions
and
Reason

729 **Early empathy** "If men and women are to understand each other, to enter into each other's nature with mutual sympathy, and to become capable of genuine comradeship, the foundation must be laid in youth."

HENRY ELLIS (1859–1939), ENGLAND

730 **Hidden barrier** "Between men and women there is no friendship possible. There is passion, enmity, worship, love, but no friendship."

OSCAR WILDE (1854–1900), IRELAND

731 **ANIMUS, ANIMA**

We all possess both feminine and masculine energies. The Swiss psychoanalyst Carl Gustav Jung (1875–1961) expressed this in terms of two complementary components of the psyche: the animus (male principle) and the anima (female principle). These may appear in our dreams as the archetypal hero or the archetypal maiden, bringing us insights from the deep part of ourselves that provides a counterpoint to our own gender. In any individual the animus/anima is influenced by the men/women of whom that person has had their earliest powerful experiences – predominantly the father or mother.

732 **Sexual chemistry** "Male and female represent the two sides of the great radical dualism. But in fact they are perpetually passing into one another. Fluid hardens to solid, solid rushes to fluid. There is no wholly masculine man, no purely feminine woman."
MARGARET FULLER (1810–1850), USA

733 **A woman's journey** "One is not born a woman, one becomes one."
SIMONE DE BEAUVOIR (1908–1986), FRANCE

734   **THE LANGUAGE OF THE HEART**
A concept developed in the 1990s by psychologists Peter Salovey and John Mayer, Emotional Intelligence is the ability to understand, articulate and manage emotions. Emotionally intelligent people recognize their feelings and are able to rein in or reframe negative emotions, such as anger, aggression and anxiety. They are equally adept at understanding the feelings of other people, and working sympathetically with them to overcome any negative emotions that they might be experiencing. Emotion will often be at odds with reason, but Emotional Intelligence helps us to avoid outright conflict.

---

735   **Private commentary** "It is not what happens to us that disturbs us, but what we think about what happens to us."
EPICTETUS (55–c.135), GREECE

736   **True empathy** "Make it your habit to listen carefully to what other people say and, as far as possible, be inside the mind of the person speaking."
MARCUS AURELIUS (121–180), ROME

737   **Shared responsibility** "Quarrels would not last long if the fault was only on one side."
FRANÇOIS, DUC DE LA ROCHEFOUCAULD (1613–1680), FRANCE

738   **Courage to continue** "Never stop because you are afraid: you are never so likely to be wrong."
FRIDTJOF NANSEN (1861–1930), NORWAY

739   **No regrets** "Grief is the agony of an instant, the indulgence of grief the blunder of a life."
BENJAMIN DISRAELI (1804–1881), ENGLAND

740   **Climate control** "A soft answer turns away wrath, but a harsh word stirs up anger."
PROVERBS 15.1

741 CHAKRAS

In certain Eastern religions, such as Hinduism, it is believed that the body has seven main energy hubs, or chakras, in a column from the base of the spine to the top of the head. Meditating on our chakras and the way in which energy flows into and out of them can help us to achieve emotional balance. The key to this balance is the "spiritual heart" – the chakra located near the heart and the well-spring of wisdom, love and poetry.

742 The eye of the beholder "We do not see things as they are. We see them as we are."

THE TALMUD

743 Driving force "Deep in their hearts, most people wish to be understood and to be cherished."

THE BUDDHA (c.563–c.483 BC), INDIA

744 **Body clock** "We live in feelings, not in figures on a sundial. We should count time in heartbeats."

ARISTOTLE (384–322 BC), GREECE

745 **Rule of thirds** "When I am getting ready to reason with a man, I spend one third of my time thinking about myself and what I am going to say and two thirds about him and what he is going to say."

ABRAHAM LINCOLN (1809–1865), USA

746 **Shifting blame** "Be not disturbed at being misunderstood; be disturbed rather at not being understanding."

CHINESE PROVERB

---

747 **PLATO'S CHARIOT**
The ancient Greek philsopher Plato (427–347 BC), in his treatise entitled *Phaedra*, describes the soul as a charioteer in control of two winged horses – one of

noble descent, handsome and gracious; the other bred of common stock, crooked and unruly. The noble horse is our reason, the ignoble horse is our appetites, from which emotions such as anger and desire are generated. The task of each of us is to steer our chariot on a straight course through life by taming our appetites and harnessing our reason, and coordinating the energies of both.

748 **The enemy within** "If you spend your life killing, you will never be rid of all your enemies. But if you quell your own anger, you will have slain your real enemy."
NAGARJUNA (2ND CENTURY), INDIA

749 **A moment of catharsis** "Sometimes a scream is better than a thesis."
RALPH WALDO EMERSON (1803–1882), USA

POSITIVE EMOTIONS

750   **Make no apologies** "Never apologize for showing feeling. When you do so, you apologize for truth."
BENJAMIN DISRAELI (1804–1881), ENGLAND

751   **Reframing your thoughts** "If you don't get everything you want, think of the things you don't get that you don't want."
OSCAR WILDE (1854–1900), IRELAND

752   **Why be an optimist?** "No pessimist ever discovered the secret of the stars or sailed an unchartered land, or opened a new doorway for the human spirit."
HELEN KELLER (1880–1968), USA

---

753   **FACING THE SUN**
Optimists see the best in any situation, and the wisdom of this approach is proven by the effects. It has even been demonstrated that optimists tend to have stronger immune

systems than pessimists, and thus have a tendency to be healthier. But even at the level of basic common sense it is clear that only those who turn to face the sun are rewarded by sunlit vistas.

---

754 **Catch some rays** "Do not anticipate trouble, or worry about what may never happen. Keep in the sunlight."
BENJAMIN FRANKLIN (1706–1790), USA

755 **No use in worrying** "Which of you by being anxious can add one cubit to your span of life?"
MATTHEW 6.27

756 **Poles apart** "A pessimist is one who makes difficulties of his opportunities and an optimist is one who makes opportunities of his difficulties."
HARRY S. TRUMAN (1884–1972), USA

757 **Stand up to your fear** "Fear arises from desire, but dissolves of its own accord when you stand firm and bear it with impartiality."
THE BUDDHA (c.563–c.483 BC), INDIA

758 **Door to door** "When one door closes, another opens, but we often look so long and so regretfully upon the closed door that we do not see the one which has opened for us."
ALEXANDER GRAHAM BELL (1847–1922), SCOTLAND/USA

759 **BECOMING AN EXPERT**
When Peter the Great of Russia wanted to introduce shipbuilding to his country, he went to England and worked in a shipyard. He might have appreciated the science of Neuro-Linguistic Programming, which involves studying the patterns of thought and conduct (including body language) of people who excel in a given field – for example, how

they would react to a particular challenge or how they would explain a setback to themselves. These findings are used to establish a model of thought and conduct that others can then mentally "set up" and use in preference to their own, perhaps less effective or less confident approach.

---

760 **The wise rush in** "Whenever you are asked if you can do a job, tell 'em, 'Certainly I can!' Then get busy and find out how to do it."
THEODORE ROOSEVELT (1858–1919), USA

761 **Snake wisdom** "As the snake's venom that spreads throughout the body is dispelled by antidotes, he who gives up anger that has arisen renounces the world of suffering, just as the snake sloughs off its old decayed skin."
THE BUDDHA (c.563–c.483 BC), INDIA

762 **Actions speak loudest** "You cannot have a proud and chivalrous spirit if your conduct is mean and paltry; for whatever your actions are, such must be your spirit."
DEMOSTHENES (c.383–322 BC), GREECE

763 **Don't explain** "The heart has its reasons, of which the mind knows nothing."
BLAISE PASCAL (1623–1662), FRANCE

---

764 **THE LIBIDO**
"Libido" in common usage means the sexual urge, but Sigmund Freud used it in a more general sense, as the psychic energy generated by a person in order to achieve personal development, or "individuation". Freud pointed out that such an instinctual energy can come into conflict with social pressures. The need to control the libido can

lead to tension and disturbance in both the individual and society. This can make for creative energy, but we need to understand where these stresses are coming from, and harmonize them within our wider being.

---

765 **The way of wonder** "There are only two ways to live your life. One is as though nothing is a miracle. The other is as though everything is a miracle."
ALBERT EINSTEIN (1879–1955), GERMANY/USA

766 **The sixth sense** "The best, most beautiful things in the world cannot be seen, or even touched. They must be felt with the heart."
HELEN KELLER (1880–1968), USA

767 **Accentuate the positive** "Positive anything is better than negative nothing."
ELBERT HUBBARD (1856–1915), USA

REASON'S ROLE

768 **Lasting peace** "The one chased away with a club comes back, but the one chased away with reason does not."
KIKUYU PROVERB, KENYA

769 **Healthy scepticism** "Digressions, objections, gleeful mockery, carefree mistrust are signs of health; everything unconditional belongs in pathology."
FRIEDRICH WILHELM NIETZSCHE (1844–1900), GERMANY

770　**Natural order** "Reason should command and desire obey."
MARCUS TULLIUS CICERO (c.106–43 BC), ROME

771　**Mind power** "The greatest discovery of my generation is that a human being can change his life by changing his attitude of mind."
WILLIAM JAMES (1842–1910), USA

772　**Leave well alone** "When you are thinking of changing something, first consider whether the change will truly bring any benefit. If not, it is best to leave things unchanged."
YOSHIDA KENKO (1283–c.1351), JAPAN

773　**Live rationally** "How fleeting and insignificant is the lot of humankind – yesterday an embryo, tomorrow a mummy or ashes. So for the hair's-breadth of time assigned to you, live rationally, and part with life cheerfully, as the ripe olive drops to the ground, extolling the season that bore it and the tree that matured it."
MARCUS AURELIUS (121–180), ROME

774 **Wrestling match** "Reason can wrestle fear and overthrow it."
EURIPIDES (480–406 BC), GREECE

775 **The shadow of reason** "Reason is like an officer when the king appears. The officer then loses his power and hides himself. Reason is the shadow cast by God; God is the sun."
JALAL AD-DIN RUMI (1207–1273), PERSIA

776 **Heart and mind** "The heart is half a prophet."
JEWISH PROVERB

777 **Fashion victims** "Our chief affliction is that we live not according to the light of reason, but after the fashion of others."
SENECA (4 BC–AD 65), ROME

778 **Muscle-bound** "We should take care not to make the intellect our god; it has, of course, powerful muscles, but no personality."
ALBERT EINSTEIN (1879–1955), GERMANY/USA

Nature
and the
Cosmos

NATURE'S BOUNTY

779 **RECHARGE IN NATURE**
The conservationist John Muir (1838–1914) urged us to "Climb the mountains and get their good tidings." It is good to immerse ourselves in natural surroundings and allow the peace of nature to flow into us. If we let the winds blow their freshness into us, and the storms their energy, our cares, as Muir said, will fall away like autumn leaves.

780 **Simply happy** "Look at the trees, look at the birds, look at the clouds, look at the stars ... and if you have eyes you will be able to see that the whole of existence is joyful. Everything is simply happy. Trees are happy for no reason; they are not going to become prime ministers or presidents and they are not going to become rich and they will never have any bank balance. Look at the flowers – for no reason. It is simply unbelievable how happy flowers are."
OSHO (1931–1990), INDIA

781 **Invest in your future** "Train up a fig tree in the way it
should go, and when you are old sit under the shade of it."
CHARLES DICKENS (1812–1870), ENGLAND

782 **The greatest service** "Whoever could make two ears
of corn, or two blades of grass, to grow upon a spot of
ground where only one grew before, would deserve better
of mankind, and do more essential service to his country,
than the whole race of politicians put together."
JONATHAN SWIFT (1667–1745), IRELAND

783 **Miracles** "All is a miracle. The stupendous order of nature,
the revolution of a hundred million of worlds round a million
of stars, the activity of light, the life of all animals, all are
grand and perpetual miracles."
VOLTAIRE (1694–1778), FRANCE

784 **All and nothing** "In my hut this spring, there is nothing –
and everything!"
SODO (1641–1715), JAPAN

785 **The fisherman's instinct**
"Listen to the sound of the river
and you will catch a trout."
IRISH PROVERB

786 **Get digging** "It will never rain
roses. When we want to have
more roses, we must plant
more roses."
GEORGE ELIOT (1819–1880),
ENGLAND

787 **Irrepressible** "Even if you drive
out nature with a pitchfork, she
will always find her way back."
HORACE (65–8 BC), ROME

NATURE'S LAWS

788 **Beyond us** "Human subtlety will never devise an invention more beautiful, more simple or more direct than does nature, because in her inventions, nothing is lacking and nothing is superfluous."
LEONARDO DA VINCI (1452–1519), ITALY

789 **Blots on the landscape** "Nature knows no indecencies; man invents them."
MARK TWAIN (1835–1910), USA

---

790 **THE DAO**
In Chinese belief, the Dao [Tao], or "Way", is the natural pattern that underlies all change and diversity in the universe – the way in which vital energy, or qi [ch'i], is endlessly created and dissolved to give rise to all phenomena. Daoism advocates literally "going with the flow" of the Dao. To achieve order and harmony in our own lives and in

the cosmos, we can learn to perceive the natural flow of the Dao and then act – or refrain from acting – in accordance with it.

---

791   **Lose yourself in the Dao** "All the fish needs is to get lost in the water. All humankind needs is to get lost in the Dao."
ZHUANGZI (C.360–C.275 BC), CHINA

792   **Nature's way** "If one way be better than another, that, you may be sure, is nature's way."
ARISTOTLE (384–322 BC), GREECE

793   **Endless wealth** "If you live according to the dictates of nature, you will never be poor; if according to the notions of humankind, you will never be rich."
SENECA (4 BC–AD 65), ROME

794   **All part of the plan** "Nature does nothing fruitlessly."
ARISTOTLE (384–322 BC), GREECE

795 Only yourself to blame "Who reaches with a clumsy hand for a rose must not complain if the thorns scratch."
HEINRICH HEINE (1797–1856), GERMANY

796 Speaking with one voice "Nature never says one thing and wisdom another."
JUVENAL (c.55–131), ROME

797 The strong, silent type "Be like a tree – strong, shady, silently productive, living only for others, letting others thrive on you, and yet keeping the environs fully clean."
SWAMI ATMANANDA (BORN c.1955), INDIA

798 All in good time "Nature does not hurry, yet everything is accomplished."
LAOZI (6TH CENTURY BC), CHINA

799 One thing leads to another "When one tugs at a single thing in nature, he finds it attached to the rest of the world."
JOHN MUIR (1838–1914), SCOTLAND/USA

800 **Unspoken rules** "Nature teaches more than she preaches. There are no sermons in stones. It is easier to get a spark out of a stone than a moral."
JOHN BURROUGHS (1837–1921), USA

801 **Self-deception** "Nature never deceives us; it is we who deceive ourselves."
JEAN-JACQUES ROUSSEAU (1712–1778), FRANCE

802 **Wild life** "Chaos often breeds life, when order breeds habit."
HENRY BROOKS ADAMS (1838–1918), USA

803 **Natural variations** "In the landscape of spring, there is neither better nor worse. The blossoming branches grow naturally, some long, some short."
ZEN SAYING

804 **Secret ingredient** "Everything in nature contains all the power of nature. Everything is made of one hidden stuff."
RALPH WALDO EMERSON (1803–1882), USA

805 **Nature's complexity** "If the Lord Almighty had consulted me before embarking upon Creation, I should have recommended something simpler."

ALFONSO X (1221–1284), KING OF LEÓN AND CASTILE, SPAIN

THE WONDER OF THE SKIES

806   **Solitary pleasure** "I would like to live in solitary confinement, far from others. Not on account of any misdemeanour I may have committed, but so that I may look in ecstasy upon the moon, as exiled poets did in days gone by."
MATSUO BASHO (1644–1694), JAPAN

807   **Uplifting** "It is clear to all that astronomy compels the soul to look upward, and draws it from the things of this world to the other."
PLATO (427–347 BC), GREECE

808   **The king of the sky** "The day of the sun is like the day of a king. It is a promenade in the morning, a sitting on the throne at noon, a pageant in the evening."
WALLACE STEVENS (1879–1955), USA

809   **Natural power** "The sun, with all those planets revolving around it and dependent on it, can still ripen a bunch of grapes as if it had nothing else in the universe to do."
GALILEO GALILEI (1564–1642), ITALY

810 **Signatures** "The Infinite has written its name on the heavens in shining stars, and on Earth in tender flowers."

JEAN PAUL RICHTER (1763–1825), GERMANY

811 **Beyond understanding** "I don't pretend to understand the Universe. It's a great deal bigger than I am."

THOMAS CARLYLE (1795–1881), SCOTLAND

812 **Of its own accord** "The sun will set without your assistance."

THE TALMUD

DISCOVERIES

813 **Ready when we are** "The universe is full of magical things patiently waiting for our wits to grow sharper."
EDEN PHILLPOTTS (1862–1960), ENGLAND

814 **New perspectives** "Discovery consists of seeing what everyone has seen and thinking what no one has thought."
ALBERT VON SZENT-GYORGYI (1893–1986), HUNGARY

815 **Hypothetical situation** "No great discovery was ever made without a bold guess."
ISAAC NEWTON (1642–1727), ENGLAND

816 **A whole world within** "We carry within us all the wonders we seek without us: there is all Africa and her prodigies in us."
THOMAS BROWNE (1605–1682), ENGLAND

817 **Rationalization** "The process of scientific discovery is, in effect, a continual flight from wonder."
ALBERT EINSTEIN (1879–1955), GERMANY/USA

818 **Total enjoyment** "You never enjoy the world aright, till the Sea itself floweth in your veins, till you are clothed with the heavens, and crowned with the stars: and perceive yourself to be the sole heir of all the world ... . Till you can sing and rejoice and delight in God, as misers do in gold, and Kings in sceptres, you never enjoy the world."

THOMAS TRAHERNE (c.1636–1674), ENGLAND

819 **Definition of physics** "It is wrong to think that the task of physics is to find out how nature is. Physics concerns what we can say about nature."

NIELS BOHR (1885–1962), DENMARK

820 **Star-gazers** "None of us sees what is before our feet: we all gaze at the stars."
MARCUS TULLIUS CICERO (c.106–43 BC), ROME

821 **A word of warning** "What can we gain by sailing to the moon if we are not able to cross the abyss that separates us from ourselves? This is the most important of all voyages of discovery, and without it, all the rest are not only useless, but disastrous."
THOMAS MERTON (1915–1968), USA

822 **Just visiting** "We are all visitors to this time, this place. We are just passing through. Our purpose here is to observe, to learn, to grow, to love, and then we return home."
AUSTRALIAN ABORIGINAL SAYING

SACRED EARTH

823 **THE SACRED TREE**
The Sacred Tree, also known as the World Tree or Tree of Life, is one of the most widely known symbols on Earth, appearing in Norse, Celtic and Indian mythologies to name but a few. It stands as an image of the cosmos, a metaphor for creation – its roots in the earth, its uppermost branches in heaven. And it offers us an image of personal growth: humanity ascending from its lower nature toward spiritual illumination, salvation, or release from the cycle of being.

824 **The kernel of creation** "The creation of a thousand forests is in one acorn."
RALPH WALDO EMERSON (1803–1882), USA

825 **A fundamental lesson** "You must teach your children that the ground beneath their feet is the ashes of your

grandfathers. So that they will respect the land, tell your children that the earth is rich with the lives of our kin. Teach your children what we have taught our children, that the earth is our mother. Whatever befalls the earth befalls the sons of the earth. If men spit upon the ground, they spit upon themselves."

CHIEF SEATTLE (c.1786–1866), SUQUAMISH NATION

826 **God's work** "I asked the whole frame of the world about my God; and he answered, 'I am not He, but He made me'."

ST AUGUSTINE OF HIPPO (354–430), NORTH AFRICA

827 **The aspiring rose** "A rose, bent by the winds and twisted by thorns, yet has its heart turned upwards."

HUNA (c.250), BABYLON

828 **The world chorus** "All life's forms are akin, yet none is like to another: they are a Choir that makes God's hidden art manifest."

JOHANN WOLFGANG VON GOETHE (1749–1832), GERMANY

829   **Everyday miracles** "I like to walk alone on country paths, rice plants and wild grasses on both sides, putting each foot down on the earth in mindfulness, knowing that I walk on the wondrous earth. In such moments, existence is a miraculous and mysterious reality. People usually consider walking on water or in thin air a miracle. But I think the real miracle is ... to walk on earth. Every day we are engaged in a miracle which we don't even recognize: a blue sky, white clouds, green leaves, the black, curious eyes of a child – our own two eyes. All is a miracle."

THICH NHAT HANH (BORN 1926), VIETNAM/FRANCE

830   **THE WORLD SOUL**
Many tribal societies believe in animism – the notion that all things (or all *natural* things) are inhabited by a spiritual life-force, corresponding to the divine. One form of animism is the belief in a "world soul" that permeates all creation. Animist peoples do

not consider themselves to be superior to other life-forms – they instinctively work in harmony with nature, rather than attempting to impose themselves on it.

---

831   **Open house** "We share the air with the forests and the water with the seas. As a body they and we are one."
THE BUDDHA (c.563–c.483 BC), INDIA

832   **Family dynamic** "Heaven is my father and Earth is my mother, and even a being as small as myself finds an intimate place in their midst. What fills the universe I look on as my own body and what directs the universe I regard as my own nature. All people are my brothers and sisters, and all things are my companions."
ZHANG ZAI (1027–1077), CHINA

833   **Gardening** "A garden grows people as well as plants."
MODERN SAYING

834 **Beyond our control** "A flower falls, even though we love it; and a weed grows, even though we do not love it."
DOGEN (1200–1253), JAPAN

835 **Inside out, outside in** "I only went out for a walk, and finally concluded to stay out till sundown, for going out, I found, was really going in."
JOHN MUIR (1838–1914), SCOTLAND/USA

836 **Invitation** "The first flower that blossomed on Earth was an invitation to the unborn song."
RABINDRANATH TAGORE (1861–1941), INDIA

837 **Conceptions of the divine** "The Theologian dreams of a God sitting above the clouds ... but we enthrone Him upon wings of the birds, on the petals of flowers, on the faces of our friends, and upon whatever we most delight in that lives upon Earth."
SAMUEL BUTLER (1835–1902), ENGLAND

ANIMAL WISDOM

838 **Spiritual companions** "What is man without the beasts? If all the beasts were gone, man would die from a great loneliness of spirit. For whatever happens to the beasts soon happens to man."
CHIEF SEATTLE (C.1786–1866), SUQUAMISH NATION

839 **The slightest difference** "Humankind differs from the animals only by a little, and most people throw that away."
CONFUCIUS (551–479 BC), CHINA

840 **God in all** "If your heart were right, then every creature would be a mirror of life and a book of holy teaching. There is no creature so small and abject but it reflects the goodness of God."
THOMAS À KEMPIS (1379–1471), GERMANY

841 **Sustainable development** "There is nothing in which the birds differ more from man than the way in which they can build and yet leave a landscape as it was before."
ROBERT LYND (1879–1949), IRELAND

842 **Animal comedy** "It is seldom that I laugh at an animal, and when I do, I usually find out afterwards that it was at myself, at the human being whom the animal has portrayed in a more or less pitiless caricature, that I have laughed."
K. LORENZ (1903–1989), AUSTRIA

843 **Just imagine** "If dogs could talk, perhaps we would find it as hard to get along with them as we do with people."
KAREL CAPEK (1890–1938), CZECHOSLOVAKIA

844 **Be like an ant** "Go to the ant, you lazybones; consider her ways, and be wise.
PROVERBS 6.6

Art and Beauty

NATURE'S BEAUTY _____

845   **Effortless beauty** "Consider the lilies of the field, how they grow; they neither toil nor spin, yet I tell you, even Solomon in all his glory was not clothed like one of these."
MATTHEW 6.28–29

846   **A shared pleasure** "I know the joy of fishes in the river through my own joy, as I go walking along the same river."
ZHUANGZI (C.360–C.275 BC), CHINA

847   **Look around** "Glance at the sun. See the moon and stars. Gaze at the beauty of the green earth. Now think."
HILDEGARD OF BINGEN (1098–1179), GERMANY

848   **Stay in touch** "Man's heart, away from nature, becomes hard."
CHIEF STANDING BEAR (1834–1908), PONCA NATION

849   **A meeting place** "Under cherry blossoms there are no strangers."
ISSA (1763–1827), JAPAN

850 **A privilege** "I once had a sparrow alight upon my shoulder for a moment, while I was hoeing in a village garden, and I felt that I was more distinguished by that circumstance than I should have been by any epaulet I could have worn."
HENRY DAVID THOREAU (1817–1862), USA

---

851 **THE INNOCENT EYE**
"I never saw an ugly thing in my life", said the great English painter John Constable (1776–1837). Looking at fine paintings, we can see how the ordinary and everyday can be made beautiful: maybe we can take the next step and see the beauty in things we take for granted or even consider ugly.

---

852 **The beholder** "Beauty is no quality in things themselves. It exists merely in the mind which contemplates them."
DAVID HUME (1711–1776), SCOTLAND

853 **A precious gift** "Youth is happy because it has the capacity to see Beauty. Anyone who keeps the ability to see Beauty never grows old."

FRANZ KAFKA (1883–1924), CZECHOSLOVAKIA

854 **Reciprocation** "Forget not that the earth delights to feel your bare feet and the winds long to play with your hair."

KAHLIL GIBRAN (1883–1931), LEBANON/USA

855 **Divine hand** "Never lose an opportunity of seeing anything that is beautiful, for beauty is God's handwriting – a wayside sacrament. Welcome it in every fair face, in every fair sky, in every fair flower, and thank God for it as a cup of blessing."

RALPH WALDO EMERSON (1803–1882), USA

856 **The heart's eye** "Man makes holy what he believes, as he makes beautiful what he loves."

ERNEST RENAN (1823–1892), FRANCE

857 BEAUTY IN VIEW
We all feel a benefit when surrounded by beautiful objects. Perhaps beauty is a sense that somehow every element in whatever we are looking at is exactly right in relation to every other. Traditionally, beauty's three hallmarks are harmony, proportion and unity.

858 Forever young "The pursuit of truth and beauty is a sphere of activity in which we are permitted to remain children all our lives."
ALBERT EINSTEIN (1879–1955), GERMANY/USA

859 Special places "Everybody needs beauty as well as bread, places to play in and pray in, where nature may heal and give strength to body and soul."
JOHN MUIR (1838–1914), SCOTLAND/USA

INSPIRATIONS _____

860 **Treasure-trove** "The most beautiful thing we can experience is the mysterious. It is the source of all true art and science."
ALBERT EINSTEIN (1879–1955), GERMANY/USA

861 **Astronomical potential** "The sight of the stars makes me dream."
VINCENT VAN GOGH (1853–1890), HOLLAND

862 **Pearl fishing** "Dive deep, O mind, dive deep in the ocean of God's beauty! If you descend to the uttermost depths, there you will find the gem of love."
BENGALI HYMN

863 **Divine dimensions** "To display his eternal attributes in their inexhaustible variety, the Lord made the green fields of time and space."
JAMI (1414–1492), PERSIA

864 **From the sublime to the judicious** "The Imagination of man is naturally sublime, delighted with whatever is remote

and extraordinary … A correct judgment observes a contrary method, and avoiding all distant and high enquiries, confines itself to common life, and to such subjects as fall under practice and experience."

DAVID HUME (1711–1776), SCOTLAND

865 **Enlightenment conductors** "I decided that it was not wisdom that enabled poets to write their poetry, but a kind of instinct or inspiration, such as you find in seers and prophets who deliver all their sublime messages without knowing in the least what they mean."

SOCRATES (469–399 BC), GREECE

866 **TOWARD PERFECTION**
Perfection is the ultimate aspiration in any field of activity; and the notion of perfection draws us on in countless ways, even though we know that this elevated goal will always remain obstinately out of reach.

The perfect picture will not be painted; the perfect symphony will not be composed. Our deepest instincts tell us that true perfection is not of this world, yet this is still the idea that inspires us to do our very best. Perfection is not the goal but the dream beyond the goal that inspires our best achievements.

---

867 **A hunger for beauty** "The pursuit of the perfect ... is the pursuit of sweetness and light."

MATTHEW ARNOLD (1822–1888), ENGLAND

868 **Paradise gained** "All the utopias will come to pass only when we grow wings and all people are changed into angels."

FYODOR DOSTOEVSKY (1821–1881), RUSSIA

869 **Deep down** "The soul is kissed by God in its innermost regions."

HILDEGARD OF BINGEN (1098–1179), GERMANY

870 THE FLASH OF AWARENESS
Satori is a Japanese word that roughly translates as "individual enlightenment". Particularly in the West, it is often used to define a flash of enhanced awareness: the moment in which everything seems intensely real and totally knowable. Traditionally, *satori* is acquired through meditation, introspection, and through mental exercises using koans, or traditional riddles. But we can also experience *satori* in the middle of some everyday activity when our minds are, apparently at least, otherwise engaged.

---

871 The open door "The soul should always stand ajar, ready to welcome the ecstatic experience."
EMILY DICKINSON (1830–1886), USA

THE HUMAN FORM

872   **Simply beautiful** "Beauty when unadorned is adorned the most."
ST JEROME (c.320–420)

873   **Dress your self** "Know, first, who you are; and then adorn yourself accordingly."
EPICTETUS (55–c.135), GREECE

874   **Haute couture** "The dress must not hang on the body but follow its lines. It must accompany its wearer and when a woman smiles the dress must smile with her."
MADELEINE VIONNET (1876–1975), FRANCE

875   **Lifelong beauty** "As we grow old, the beauty steals inward."
RALPH WALDO EMERSON (1803–1882), USA

876   **The plain truth** "The Lord prefers common-looking people. That is the reason he makes so many of them."
ABRAHAM LINCOLN (1809–1865), USA

877 **CATEGORIES OF VIRTUE**
When Pope Gregory the Great (c. 540–604) defined the Seven Deadly Sins, he also laid down a set of seven virtues. These are: Faith, Hope, Charity, Fortitude, Justice, Prudence and Temperance. In contrast, Buddhists aspire to six "perfections": Generosity, Morality, Patience, Energy, Meditation and Wisdom.

---

878 **Nobility in action** "If abuses are destroyed, man must destroy them. If slaves are freed, man must free them. If new truths are discovered, man must discover them. If the naked are clothed, if the hungry are fed, if justice is done, if labour is rewarded, if superstition is driven from the mind, if the defenceless are protected and if the right finally triumphs, all must be the work of man. The grand victories of the future must be won by man, and by man alone."
ROBERT G. INGERSOLL (1833–1899), USA

879 **Time to be a hero** "A hero is no braver than an ordinary man, but he is braver five minutes longer."
RALPH WALDO EMERSON
(1803–1882), USA

880 **Constant companions** "They are never alone that are accompanied with noble thoughts."
PHILIP SIDNEY (1554–1586), ENGLAND

881 **Songs of affirmation** "Don't waste yourself in rejection, nor bark against the bad, but chant the beauty of the good."
RALPH WALDO EMERSON
(1803–1882), USA

THE ARTIST'S CALLING _____

882 **Liberating the soul** "There is not a single true work of art that has not in the end added to the inner freedom of each person who has known and loved it."
ALBERT CAMUS (1913–1960), FRANCE

883 **Call and response** "What is art? It is the response of man's creative Soul to the call of the Real."
RABINDRANATH TAGORE (1861–1941), INDIA

884 **Guiding principle** "Beauty of style and harmony and grace and good rhythm depends on simplicity."
PLATO (427–347 BC), GREECE

885 **Art and utility** "Have nothing in your house that you do not know to be useful, or do not believe to be beautiful."
WILLIAM MORRIS (1834–1896), ENGLAND

886 **A radical view** "Art is either plagiarism or revolution."
PAUL GAUGUIN (1848–1903), FRANCE

887 Sculpture's law "The more the marble wastes, the more the statue grows."
MICHELANGELO BUONARROTI (1475–1564), ITALY

888 Sensing the way "A good traveller has no fixed plans and is not intent upon arriving. A good artist lets his intuition lead him wherever it wants."
LAOZI (6TH CENTURY BC), CHINA

889 The artistic medium "Painting is the intermediate somewhat between a thought and a thing."
SAMUEL TAYLOR COLERIDGE (1772–1834), ENGLAND

890 Tone poem "A painting is a poem without words."
HORACE (65–8 BC), ROME

891 Brush doubts aside "If you hear a voice within you saying, 'You are no painter', *then paint by all means*, lad, and that voice will be silenced, but only by working."
VINCENT VAN GOGH (1853–1890), HOLLAND

892   **Artistic licence** "There is no rule that may not be broken in the pursuit of a greater beauty."
LUDWIG VAN BEETHOVEN (1770–1827), GERMANY

---

893   **THE STONES OF VENICE**
Visiting a Renaissance church in Venice, the art critic John Ruskin was annoyed to find that the elaborate sculptures placed against its walls were one-sided only. The backs, hidden from view, had been only roughly modelled. These works, he argued, had been offered to God, not to the general public, and God could see the backs just as well as the fronts.

---

894   **Great expectations** "When love and skill go together, expect a masterpiece."
JOHN RUSKIN (1819–1900), ENGLAND

895 **True lies** "We all know that Art is not truth. Art is a lie that makes us realize the truth, at least the truth that is given to us to understand."
PABLO PICASSO (1881–1973), SPAIN

896 **Second-guessing** "The artist's object is to make things not as nature makes them, but as she *would* make them."
RAPHAEL (1483–1520), ITALY

897 **A perfect match**
"Truth is within the reach of a wise man. Beauty can be reached by a sensitive heart. They belong to each other."
FRIEDRICH SCHILLER (1759–1805), GERMANY

MUSIC AND POETRY _____

898 **Connecting with the unknown** "Music! You speak to me of things which in all my endless life I have not found, and shall not find."

JEAN PAUL RICHTER (1763–1825), GERMANY

899 **Body and soul** "Music is the mediator between the spiritual and the sensual life."

LUDWIG VAN BEETHOVEN (1770–1827), GERMANY

900 **Harmony from discord** "Medicine to produce health must examine disease; and music, to create harmony, must investigate discord."

PLUTARCH (46–120), GREECE

901 **Making waves** "Music is the movement of sound to reach the soul for the education of its virtue. ... Music is a moral law. It gives soul to the universe, wings to the mind, flight to the imagination, a charm to sadness, and life to everything."

PLATO (427–347 BC), GREECE

902 **An intellectual note** "It had never occurred to me before that music and thinking are so much alike. In fact, you could say music is another way of thinking, or maybe thinking is another kind of music."

URSULA K. LE GUIN (BORN 1929), USA

903 **THE ZONE**
The "zone" is the name commonly given to a state of complete mental immersion in a creative activity. Once "in the zone", you lose awareness of yourself, the passing of time and anything else that is unconnected with the project in hand. After leaving the zone you will look back with surprise at what you have created.

904   **Romantic wisdom** "Poetry is the spontaneous overflow of powerful feelings: It takes its origin from emotion recollected in tranquillity."

WILLIAM WORDSWORTH (1770–1850), ENGLAND

905   **Dreamer's charter** "Too much sanity may be madness and the maddest of all, to see life as it is and not as it should be."

MIGUEL DE CERVANTES (1547–1616), SPAIN

906   **Poetry and history** "Poetry is finer and more philosophical than history; for poetry expresses the universal, and history only the particular."

ARISTOTLE (384–322 BC), GREECE

907   **Naked beauty** "Poetry redeems from decay the visitations of the divinity in man: it strips the veil of familiarity from the world, and lays bare the naked and sleeping beauty which is the spirit of its forms."

PERCY BYSSHE SHELLEY (1792–1822), ENGLAND

908   **Next to God** "None merits the name of Creator but God and the poet."
TORQUATO TASSO (1544–1595), ITALY

909   **A paradox** "A poet, even one who has never experienced grief, can describe a broken heart and be believed; yet one who truly mourns has not the skill to put sorrow into words."
ANCIENT SANSKRIT VERSE, INDIA

910   **Waxing lyrical** "At the touch of love everyone becomes a poet."
PLATO (427–347 BC), GREECE

911   **Thankless task** "Poets are the unacknowledged legislators of mankind."
PERCY BYSSHE SHELLEY (1792–1822), ENGLAND

912   **Poetry appreciation society** "To have great poets, there must be great audiences."
WALT WHITMAN (1819–1892), USA

A Better World

SURVIVAL

913   **Love and compassion** "We humans have existed in our present form for about a hundred thousand years. I believe that if during this time the human mind had been primarily controlled by anger and hatred, our overall population would have decreased. But today, despite all our wars, we find that the human population is greater than ever. This clearly indicates to me that love and compassion predominate in the world. And this is why unpleasant events are "news"; compassionate activities are so much a part of daily life that they are taken for granted and, therefore, largely ignored."

TENZIN GYATSO, 14TH DALAI LAMA (BORN 1934), TIBET

914   **Positive impetus** "Injustice, poverty, slavery, ignorance – these may be cured by reform or revolution. But men do not live only by fighting evils. They live by positive goals, individual and collective, a vast variety of them, seldom predictable, sometimes incompatible."

ISAIAH BERLIN (1909–1997), ENGLAND

915 **Adaptability** "It is not the strongest of the species that survives, nor the most intelligent. It is the one that is the most adaptable to change."
CHARLES DARWIN (1809–1882), ENGLAND

916 **Inflammatory** "It would indeed be a tragedy if the history of the human race proved to be nothing more than the story of an ape playing with a box of matches on a petroleum dump."
DAVID ORMSBY-GORE (1918–1985), ENGLAND

917 **Cosmic perspective** "I do not value any view of the universe into which man and the institutions of man enter very largely and absorb much of the attention. Man is but the place where I stand, and the prospect hence is infinite."
HENRY DAVID THOREAU (1817–1862), USA

918 **Prerequisite** "Our civilization cannot survive materially unless it be redeemed spiritually."
WOODROW WILSON (1856–1924), USA

919 Rallying cry "The problems that exist in the world today cannot be solved by the level of thinking that created them."
ALBERT EINSTEIN (1879–1955), GERMANY/USA

920 Prudent investment "It is the part of wise men to preserve themselves today for tomorrow, and not risk all in one day."
MIGUEL DE CERVANTES (1547–1616), SPAIN

921 Law of nature "What does not grow, declines."
RABBI HILLEL (1ST CENTURY BC), JERUSALEM

RESPONSIBILITY

922   **Culinary guidance** "Governing a great people is like cooking a small fish. It should not be overdone."

LAOZI (6TH CENTURY BC), CHINA

923   **The price of a privilege** "I believe that every right implies a responsibility; every opportunity, an obligation; every possession, a duty."

JOHN D. ROCKEFELLER JR (1874–1960), USA

---

924   **MAAT**
The ancient Egyptians believed that the universe was created in a state of *maat* – perfect order or truth. *Maat*, which was revered as a powerful goddess, had to be maintained against the dark forces of chaos. For the king, upholding *maat* meant defending the people against foreign enemies and disorder. For all people, living in accordance with *maat* meant social and

moral justice: the powerful were not to exploit the weak, and all people had to strive to live in harmony with the world and one another. This exchange of rights and responsibilities between ruler and subjects evokes a workable political system that is thoroughly relevant to modern times.

---

925   **A shared responsibility** "You will be truly free when you learn to be impartial and undeterred from following the dictates of your conscience. This is the way of *maat*."
ANCIENT EGYPTIAN TEMPLE INSCRIPTION

926   **Spurious distinction** "What difference does it make to the dead, the orphans, and the homeless, whether the mad destruction is wrought under the name of totalitarianism or the holy name of liberty or democracy?"
MAHATMA GANDHI (1869–1948), INDIA

927 **A three-prong fork** "The pursuit of politics is religion, morality and poetry, all in one."
MADAME DE STAËL (1766–1817), FRANCE

928 **Entering public life** "When a man assumes a public trust, he should consider himself as public property."
THOMAS JEFFERSON (1743–1826), USA

929 **Negative neutrality** "If you are neutral in situations of injustice, you have chosen the side of the oppressor. If an elephant has its foot on the tail of a mouse and you say that you are neutral, the mouse will not appreciate your neutrality."
DESMOND TUTU (BORN 1931), SOUTH AFRICA

930 **Embarrassment of riches** "In a country well governed, poverty is something to be ashamed of. In a country ill governed, wealth is something to be ashamed of."
CONFUCIUS (551–479 BC), CHINA

931 **Making a difference** "The philosophers have only interpreted the world: the point is to change it."
KARL MARX (1818–1883), GERMANY

932 **A real challenge** "Nearly all men can stand adversity, but if you want to test a man's character, give him power."
ABRAHAM LINCOLN (1809–1865), USA

933 **Civil disobedience** "We cannot, by total reliance on law, escape the duty to judge right and wrong ... There are good laws and there are occasionally bad laws, and it conforms to the highest traditions of a free society to offer resistance to bad laws, and to disobey them."
ALEXANDER M. BICKEL (1924–1974), USA

934 **Something in return** "It is every man's obligation to put back into the world at least the equivalent of what he takes out of it."
ALBERT EINSTEIN (1879–1955), GERMANY/USA

935   **Social anatomy** "Justice is the ligament which holds civilized beings and civilized nations together."
DANIEL WEBSTER (1782–1852), USA

936   **Personal intervention** "'I must do something' always solves more problems than 'Something must be done.'"
ANONYMOUS MODERN SAYING

937   **Democratic duty** "People often say that, in a democracy, decisions are made by a majority of the people. Of course, that is not true. Decisions are made by a majority of those who make themselves heard and who vote – a very different thing."
WALTER H. JUDD (1898–1994), USA

938   **Going with the flow** "No snowflake in an avalanche ever feels responsible."
VOLTAIRE (1694–1778), FRANCE

PEACE

939 **Offer of service** "Lord, make me an instrument of thy peace. Where there is hatred, let me sow love."

ST FRANCIS OF ASSISI (C.1181–1226), ITALY

940 **The noble warrior** "The way of the warrior has been misunderstood as a means to kill and destroy others. Those who seek competition are making a grave mistake. To smash, injure or destroy is the worst sin a human being can commit. The true way of the warrior is to prevent slaughter – it is the art of peace, the power of love."

MORIHEI UESHIBA (1883–1969), JAPAN

941 **Strength in unity** "A farmer called together his quarrelsome sons and told them each to bring a stick and lay it before him. After placing the sticks alongside one another and binding them, the farmer challenged his sons, one after the other, to pick up the bundle and break it. They all tried, but in vain. Then the farmer untied the bundle and gave each son a stick to break, one by one. They did this with the greatest of ease. Finally the father said: 'So you see,

my sons, as long as you remain united, you are a match for
anything. But differ and be divided, and you are undone.'"
AESOP (620–560 BC), GREECE

942 **Peace at all costs** "For me the most unfair peace is
preferable to the most righteous war."
MARCUS TULLIUS CICERO (c.106–43 BC), ROME

943 **A JUST WAR**
St Augustine (354–430) and, many centuries
later, St Thomas Aquinas (1224–1274)
developed the concept of the "just war" to
address the question of when, if ever, it is
right to take arms. Above all, there must be
a "just cause" – for example, few would deny
a nation the right to defend itself against
invaders. More problematic issues include:
can pre-emptive strikes be valid? and is it
ever legitimate to target non-combatants?

944 **Best of intentions** "We do not seek peace in order to be at war, but we go to war that we may have peace. Be peaceful, therefore, in warring, so that you may vanquish those whom you war against, and bring them to the prosperity of peace."

ST AUGUSTINE OF HIPPO (354–430), NORTH AFRICA

945 **Personal contribution** "It is not by going out for a demonstration against nuclear missiles that we can bring about peace. It is with our capacity of smiling, breathing, and being peace that we can make peace."

THICH NHAT HANH (BORN 1926), VIETNAM/FRANCE

946 **The peacemaker's prayer** "Praise be to the Lord of the Universe who has created us and made us into tribes and nations, that we may know each other, not that we may despise each other. If the enemy incline toward peace do you also incline toward peace, and trust in God, for the Lord it is that hears and knows all things. And the servants of God

Most Gracious are those who walk on the Earth in humility, and when we address them, we say, 'Peace'."

ISLAMIC PRAYER

947 **Justifiable defence** "Fight in the way of God with those who fight with you, but do not aggress, for God does not love aggressors."

THE QURAN

948 **The parent's sacrifice** "If there must be trouble let it be in my day, that my child may have peace."

THOMAS PAINE (1737–1809), ENGLAND

949 **Cohabitation** "Adapt yourself to the things among which your lot has been cast, and love sincerely the fellow creatures with whom destiny has ordained that you shall live."

MARCUS AURELIUS (121–180), ROME

950 **Above and beyond** "Nonviolence is the supreme law."

HINDU SAYING

951   **The courage of the dove** "Peace ... demands greater heroism than war. It demands greater fidelity to the truth and a much more perfect purity of conscience."

THOMAS MERTON (1915–1968), USA

952   **Compulsion or compassion?** "A peace that comes from fear and not from the heart is the opposite of peace."

GERSONIDES (RABBI LEVI BEN GERSHON) (1288–1344), FRANCE

953   **The art of peace** "The practice of peace and reconciliation is one of the most vital and artistic of human actions."

THICH NHAT HANH (BORN 1926), VIETNAM/FRANCE

954   **Wishful thinking?** "There will one day spring from the brain of science a machine or force so fearful in its potentialities, so absolutely terrifying, that even man, the fighter, who will dare torture and death in order to inflict torture and death, will be appalled, and so abandon war forever."

THOMAS EDISON (1847–1931), USA

955 VICTORIOUS NON-VIOLENCE
The Sanskrit term *satyagraha* has been used since the days of Mahatma Gandhi (1869–1948) to denote a policy of passive resistance to oppression. But Gandhi himself gave the term a far wider meaning, stressing its three elements of truth, refusal to do injury, and willingness to sacrifice oneself. To him, it involved vindication of truth, not by inflicting suffering, but by being prepared oneself to suffer. It was not a philosophy for victims: in Gandhi's view, a person adopting *satyagraha* was not only unbeatable but already victorious.

---

956 Sweat and blood "The more we sweat in peace, the less we bleed in war."

VIJAYA LAKSHMI PANDIT (1900–1990), INDIA

957 **Better to lose** "There are some defeats more triumphant than victories."
MICHEL DE MONTAIGNE (1533–1592), FRANCE

958 **The perfect guest** "Whatever house you enter, first say, 'Peace to this house.'"
LUKE 10.5

959 **Against separatism** "When you call yourself an Indian or a Muslim or a Christian or a European, or anything else, you are being violent. Do you see why it is violent? Because you are separating yourself from the rest of mankind. When you separate yourself by belief, by nationality, by tradition, it breeds violence."

JIDDU KRISHNAMURTI (1895–1986), INDIA

960 **At peace, at home** "Peace, like charity, begins at home."

FRANKLIN D. ROOSEVELT (1882–1945), USA

---

961 **TOOLS OF PEACEMAKING**
Native Americans provided a form and ritual for establishing peace, including the "pipe of peace" and the ceremony of burying the axe. Like raising the flag of truce, such procedures make it easier for the peacemaker to work. At a personal level, we also use certain

accepted gestures or actions as a peace overture when we wish to resolve a conflict with, for example, a loved one. However, these signals are only a declaration of intent: qualities such as patience, empathy and understanding are needed to build a lasting peace.

---

962   **A peaceful disposition** "Peace is not the absence of war: it is a virtue; a state of mind; a disposition for benevolence ... and justice."

BENEDICT DE SPINOZA (1632–1677), HOLLAND

EQUALITY

963   **Fatal delusion** "A feeling of superiority is a sign of failure."
YOSHIDA KENKO (1283–c.1351), JAPAN

---

964   **THE STATUS OF SERVICE**
In times past the number of servants someone
had was a telling measure of social standing.
But in fact a truer valuation of a person is
how many others they themselves serve.

---

965   **Levelling up** "The defect of equality is that we only desire it
with our superiors."
HENRI BECQUE (1837–1899), FRANCE

966   **Imposing equality** "Democracy is a charming form of
government, full of variety and disorder, and dealing
with all on an equal footing, whether in reality they be
equals or not."
PLATO (427–347 BC), GREECE

967   **Checkmate** "Once the game is over, the king and the pawn go back in the same box."
ITALIAN PROVERB

968   **Fine line** "No man is above the law, and no man is below it."
THEODORE ROOSEVELT (1858–1919), USA

969   **Familiarity** "I am a human being. Nothing human is alien to me."
TERENCE (185–159 BC), ROME

970   **Notions of equality** "There is all the difference in the world between treating people equally and attempting to make them equal."
FRIEDRICH AUGUST HAYEK (1899–1992), AUSTRIA

971   **Food chain** "Life lives on life. We all eat and are eaten. Forgetting this, we weep; remembering this, we nourish one another."
THE BUDDHA (C.563–C.483 BC), INDIA

972 **Solidarity** "Years ago I recognized my kinship with all living things, and I made up my mind that I was not one bit better than the meanest on the Earth. I said then and I say now, that while there is a lower class, I am in it; while there is a criminal element, I am of it; while there is a soul in prison, I am not free."

EUGENE DEBS (1855–1926), USA

973 **An end to exploitation** "Every man is to be respected as an absolute end in himself; and it is a crime against the dignity that belongs to him as a human being to use him as a mere means for some external purpose."

IMMANUEL KANT (1724–1804), GERMANY

974 **Unfair game** "There is something wrong in a government where they who do the most have the least. There is something wrong when honesty wears a rag, and rascality a robe; when the loving, the tender, eat a crust, while the infamous sit at banquets."

ROBERT G. INGERSOLL (1833–1899), USA

975 **All the same** "I think the king is but a man, as I am;
the violet smells to him as it doth to me."
WILLIAM SHAKESPEARE (1564–1616), ENGLAND

CONSERVATION

976 Firm footing "What is the use of a house if you haven't got a tolerable planet to put it on?"

HENRY DAVID THOREAU (1817–1862), USA

977 The forest's prayer "I am the heat of your hearth on the cold winter nights, the friendly shade screening you from the summer sun, and my fruits are refreshing draughts quenching your thirst as you journey on. I am the beam that holds your house, the board of your table, the bed on which you lie, and the timber that builds your boat. I am the handle of your hoe, the door of your homestead, the wood of your cradle, the shell of your coffin. I am the bread of kindness and the floor of beauty. You who pass by, listen to my prayer: do me no harm."

TRADITIONAL PORTUGUESE PRAYER

978 Dangerous precedent "We can do without any article of luxury we have never had; but, when once obtained, it is not in human nature to surrender it voluntarily."

SAMUEL CHANDLER HALIBURTON (1796–1865), USA

979 Sun shock "When a tree falls there is no shade."
LAOZI (6TH CENTURY BC), CHINA

980 Next generation "A true conservationist is a man who knows that the world is not given by his fathers but borrowed from his children."
J.J. AUDUBON (1785–1851), USA

981 GAIA
The Gaia Hypothesis, formulated in the 1960s by the British scientist James Lovelock, sees our planet as a single living organism called Gaia, formed from a collection of sentient and non-sentient parts, and constantly regulating itself to maintain its biochemical balance. The Earth is likened to a body: its oceans and rivers are its blood vessels and the atmosphere is its lungs. Personifying the Earth in this way, as a cosmic being, makes

it seem automatically more sacred: the damage we have done to the rainforest, for example, becomes a terrifying milestone of destruction – as if we had taken up a length of cord and used it to strangle ourselves.

---

982 **Self-defeating** "Modern man often talks of the battle with nature, forgetting that if he ever won the battle, he would be on the losing side."
ERNST F. SCHUMACHER (1911–1977), GERMANY

983 **Mission and prayer** "You and I and everything in the universe are part of the infinite flow of the divine love. When we see this, we acknowledge that this same benevolence binds together all creation. When we harmonize with life we come into accord with the part of God that flows through everything. That all life be nurtured and protected is at once our mission and our prayer."
MORIHEI UESHIBA (1883–1969), JAPAN

984   **Precedence** "The world owes you nothing. It was here first."
MARK TWAIN (1835–1910), USA

985   **Return to nature** "I see humanity now as one vast plant, needing for its highest fulfillment only love, the natural blessings of the great outdoors, and intelligent crossing and selection. In the span of my own lifetime I have observed such wondrous progress in plant evolution that I look forward optimistically to a healthy, happy world as soon as its children are taught the principles of simple and rational living. We must return to nature and nature's god."
LUTHER BURBANK (1849–1926), USA

FREEDOM

986 **FREEDOM OF THOUGHT**
Differences of opinion are the natural
by-products of a democratic society, and
freedom of thought, conscience and religion
is well established as a precious right that
any such society must preserve for all its
members. One of the great challenges
of modern times is to ensure that such
liberties remain unviolated while protecting
societies from the violence brought by the
rise of intolerance.

---

987 **Matter of principle** "I detest what you write, but I would
give my life to make it possible for you to continue to write."
VOLTAIRE (1694–1778), FRANCE

988 **Deeper impression** "Freedom suppressed, then regained,
bites with keener fangs that freedom never endangered."
MARCUS TULLIUS CICERO (C.106–43 BC), ROME

989 **Special relationship** "Freedom and love go together. Love is not a reaction. If I love you because you love me, that is mere trade, a thing to be bought in the market; it is not love. To love is not to ask anything in return, not even to feel that you are giving something – and it is only such love that can know freedom."
JIDDU KRISHNAMURTI (1895–1986), INDIA

990 **Phantoms** "Enlighten the people, generally, and tyranny and oppressions of body and mind will vanish like spirits at the dawn of day."
THOMAS JEFFERSON (1743–1826), USA

991 **New order** "He that is kind is free, though he be a slave; he that is cruel is a slave, though he be a king."
ST AUGUSTINE OF HIPPO (354–430), NORTH AFRICA

992 **Dirty work** "One should never put on one's best trousers to go out to fight for freedom."
HENRIK IBSEN (1828–1906), NORWAY

993 **Institutionalized** "Most people do not really want freedom, because freedom involves responsibility, and most people are frightened of responsibility."
SIGMUND FREUD (1856–1939), AUSTRIA

994 **The mother of oppression** "Necessity is the plea for every infringement of human freedom. It is the argument of tyrants; it is the creed of slaves."
WILLIAM PITT (1759–1806), ENGLAND

995 **THE SOCIAL CONTRACT**
The Swiss-born French philosopher Jean-Jacques Rousseau used the term "social contract" to describe the ideal relationship between the individual and society. According to Rousseau, we can live freely only by handing over our rights to the community and allowing ourselves to be governed by the "general will" – the

combined and unanimous will of the people. Those who oppose the general will should be overruled; in Rousseau's words, everyone should be "forced to be free".

---

996 **One and all** "The freedom of all is essential to my freedom."
MIKHAIL BAKUNIN (1814–1876), RUSSIA

997 **Freedom of choice** "Freedom lies only in our innate capacity to choose between different sorts of bondage: bondage to desire or self-regard, or bondage to the light that lightens all our lives."
SRI MADHAVA ASHISH (1920–1997), SCOTLAND/INDIA

998 **Concealed ties** "Man is born free, and everywhere he is in chains. One man thinks himself the master of others, but remains more of a slave than they are."
JEAN-JACQUES ROUSSEAU (1712–1778), SWITZERLAND/FRANCE

999 **Independent opinion** "Freedom for supporters of the government only, for members of one party only – no matter how big its membership may be – is no freedom at all. Freedom is always freedom for the man who thinks differently."

ROSA LUXEMBURG (1870–1919), POLAND/GERMANY

1000 **Making our own way** "Where would our divine freedom be if external nature protected us like helpless children, led by the hand? No, external nature must deny us everything so that the happiness we achieve is wholly our own independent creation."

RUDOLF STEINER (1861–1925), AUSTRIA/HUNGARY

1001 **The finished article** "Who then is free? The one who wisely is lord of himself, terrified by neither poverty nor death nor captivity; who is strong in resisting his appetites and in shunning honours, and complete in himself."

HORACE (65–8 BC), ROME

INDEX

ACKNOWLEDGMENTS

The publishers wish to thank the following for their kind permission to reproduce the copyright material in this book. Every effort has been made to trace copyright holders, but if anyone has been omitted we apologize and will, if informed, make corrections in any future edition.

References are to "pearl numbers". **55** from *The Gospel of Sri Ramakrishna*, as translated by Swami Nikhilananda (Ramakrishna-Vivekananda Center of New York, 1942); **63** from *The Second Sin* by Thomas Szász (Anchor Books, 1973). Copyright © Thomas Szász. Reprinted by permission of McIntosh and Otis, Inc.; **102** from "Modern Fiction" by Virginia Woolf (Times Literary Supplement, 1919). Reprinted by permission of the Society of Authors as the literary representative of the estate of Virginia Woolf; **103** from *The Essence of Buddhism* by Daisetz Suzuki (The Buddhist Society, 1946). Copyright © The Buddhist Society; **105** from *How to Know God* by Deepak Chopra (Three Rivers Press, 2001); **127** attributed to Rabindranath Tagore, precise source unknown. Reprinted by permission of Visva-Bharati University; **134** and **140** from *The Gospel of Sri Ramakrishna*, as translated by Swami Nikhilananda (Ramakrishna-Vivekananda Center of New York, 1942); **174** attributed to Rabindranath Tagore, precise source unknown. Reprinted by permission of Visva-Bharati University; **225** copyright © DBP; **229** from *Transformation and Healing* by Thich Nhat Hanh (Parallax Press, 1990). Copyright © Parallax Press; **250** from *The Four Loves* by C.S. Lewis (Collins, 1960). Copyright © C.S. Lewis Pte. Ltd.; **263** copyright © DBP; **324** attributed to C.S. Lewis, precise source unknown. Copyright © C.S. Lewis Pte. Ltd.; **349** copyright © DBP; **361** from *Justice and Mercy* by Reinhold Niebuhr (Harper and Row, 1974). Copyright © Elisabeth Sifton; **454** from *The Human Revolution* by Daisaku Ikeda (Weatherhill, 1972). Reprinted by permission of Shambhala Publications; **455** from *The Myth of Freedom and the Way of Meditation* by Chögyam Trungpa Rinpoche (Shambhala, 1976). Reprinted by permission of Shambhala Publications; **456** from "A Servant to Servants" from the *Poetry of Robert Frost* edited by Edward Connery Lathem. Copyright 1958 by